# 100

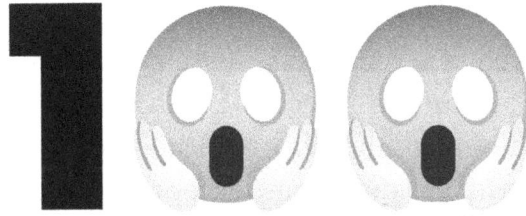

# MIND-BLOWING STORIES

*Fascinating Stories of the Strange,*
*Surprising, and Unbelievable*

## FELIX GRAYSON

**MINDSPARK**
PUBLISHING

# CONTENTS

# BEFORE WE DIVE IN...

D id you know that this is just **one** of many **mind-blowing** books waiting to be discovered?

What if I told you there's a **world of jaw-dropping, unbelievable, and downright bizarre facts** across **sports, science, history, mysteries, and more**—each one packed with stories that will **challenge what you thought you knew?**

## EVER WONDERED WHAT IT'S LIKE TO...

- Witness **record-breaking Olympic moments** that defy human limits?

- Explore **real-life conspiracy theories** that sound too wild to be true?

- Discover **unsolved mysteries** that still leave experts baffled?

- Learn about **billionaires, stock market crashes, and money secrets?**

- Find out how **robots, AI, and space travel are**

shaping the future?

- Experience the **most extreme sports, legendary battles, and shocking events?**

This is just the beginning. The **100 Mind-Blowing series** covers it **all.**

## WANT TO SEE WHAT'S NEXT?

Go to **FelixGrayson.com** and explore the **growing collection** of books and audiobooks that will **entertain, amaze, and keep you coming back for more.**

FelixGrayson.com

**Curiosity doesn't stop here—this is just the beginning.** What will blow your mind next?

# INTRODUCTION

Welcome to *100 Mind-Blowing Stories*, a collection designed to tickle your curiosity and leave you saying, "Wait, what?" From strange historical happenings to unsolved mysteries, this book is packed with tales that are as fascinating as they are unbelievable.

Have you ever wondered what caused a molasses wave to wreak havoc on a city? Or why an entire village might vanish without a trace? How about the time a war was waged—not against humans, but against emus? These are just a few of the stories waiting for you inside. Each tale has been carefully chosen to surprise, delight, and perhaps even stump your trivia-loving friends.

Whether you're here for a quick escape, a quirky conversation starter, or a treasure trove of fascinating facts, this book has you covered. Read it from cover to cover, or flip to a random page and see where curiosity takes you. There's no right or wrong way to enjoy this journey through the strange, surprising, and unbelievable.

So grab your favorite beverage, find a cozy spot,

and get ready to explore some of the most mind-blowing stories the world has to offer. Who knows? By the end, you might even have a few jaw-dropping tales of your own to share. Let's dive in!

# THE MYSTERY OF THE LIGHTHOUSE KEEPERS

In December 1900, a chilling mystery unfolded in the remote Flannan Isles of Scotland. Three lighthouse keepers—Thomas Marshall, James Ducat, and Donald McArthur—vanished without a trace from the Eilean Mòr lighthouse, leaving behind a mystery that has confounded investigators and storytellers for over a century.

The lighthouse was critical for guiding ships through the treacherous waters of the North Atlantic. When the relief crew arrived on December 26, they were met with an eerie silence. The lighthouse was operational, but there were no keepers in sight. Inside, the table was set for a meal that was never eaten, a chair was

overturned, and the clock had stopped ticking. Most disturbingly, the logbook hinted at growing unease among the keepers.

Marshall, the assistant keeper, had written about severe storms battering the island and noted that Ducat was unusually quiet while McArthur—a hardened sailor—was reportedly crying. Yet, no storms were recorded in the area during those dates. The final entry, dated December 15, cryptically read: "Storm ended, sea calm. God is over all."

An investigation revealed no signs of foul play. Theories ranged from a rogue wave sweeping the men away to alien abductions and even madness-induced violence. However, no definitive evidence has ever surfaced.

To this day, the disappearance of the Flannan Isles lighthouse keepers remains one of the sea's most enduring mysteries, leaving us to wonder what truly happened to the men who vanished into the void.

# THE GREAT EMU WAR: A BATTLE DOWN UNDER

In 1932, Australia waged war against an unlikely foe—emus. These large, flightless birds, native to the country, were wreaking havoc on farmlands in Western Australia. Following a population boom, thousands of emus migrated to the region, trampling crops and frustrating farmers who had already suffered through the Great Depression.

The government responded by deploying soldiers armed with machine guns to combat the avian invaders. Led by Major G.P.W. Meredith, the campaign seemed destined for success. However, the emus proved to be surprisingly agile and resilient. They dodged bullets with uncanny speed, and their scattered movements made them difficult targets. Despite several

attempts, the military only managed to kill around 1,000 emus—barely a dent in the population.

Newspaper headlines mocked the campaign, labeling it "The Great Emu War" and declaring the emus the victors. Frustrated, the government eventually withdrew the military, leaving farmers to fend for themselves. The failed operation highlighted the emus' adaptability and the limitations of human ingenuity in the face of nature.

Today, the Great Emu War is remembered as a bizarre yet humorous chapter in Australia's history—a tale of man versus bird where the birds emerged triumphant.

# PTOLEMY AND THE MAP THAT SHAPED THE WORLD

In the second century AD, the Greek astronomer and geographer Claudius Ptolemy created a map that would influence humanity's understanding of the world for over a thousand years. Ptolemy's map wasn't perfect—it missed entire continents, including the Americas and Australia—but it introduced revolutionary concepts like latitude, longitude, and the idea of a spherical Earth.

While earlier civilizations like the Babylonians and Egyptians used crude maps for local navigation, Ptolemy's map provided a more comprehensive, global perspective. It combined scientific observations with reports from traders and explorers, resulting in an ambitious attempt

to chart the known world. The map even hinted at the existence of terra incognita—"unknown lands"—which would fuel the imaginations of future explorers.

Ptolemy's ideas were rediscovered during the Renaissance, a time of renewed interest in science and exploration. His work became the foundation for navigational advances, inspiring figures like Christopher Columbus. However, Ptolemy also made errors that persisted for centuries—his map vastly underestimated the Earth's size, leading explorers like Columbus to believe Asia was much closer than it was.

Despite its flaws, Ptolemy's map was a groundbreaking achievement. It bridged the gap between ancient knowledge and modern science, reminding us of humanity's enduring desire to understand and explore the world.

# THE DANCING PLAGUE OF 1518

In the sweltering summer of 1518, the citizens of Strasbourg, France, found themselves in the grip of a bizarre and deadly phenomenon: people dancing uncontrollably in the streets. What began with one woman's frenzied movements soon spread to dozens, and eventually hundreds, of townspeople, all unable to stop their relentless dancing.

Witnesses described scenes of exhaustion and despair as dancers collapsed from fatigue or even died from heart attacks and strokes. Local authorities, desperate for a solution, consulted physicians, who attributed the outbreak to "hot blood," a medical theory of the time. Their unconventional remedy? More dancing. They erected stages, hired musicians, and encouraged the afflicted to "dance it out."

But rather than resolving the crisis, these efforts only fueled the madness. The dancing continued for weeks, leaving a trail of bewilderment and tragedy.

Modern historians and scientists have speculated about the cause of this so-called "Dancing Plague." Some suggest mass hysteria, brought on by stress and superstition, while others point to ergot poisoning—a condition caused by consuming moldy rye that can induce hallucinations and convulsions. However, no theory fully explains why the phenomenon spread so widely and affected so many.

The Dancing Plague of 1518 remains one of history's most peculiar medical mysteries. Was it a physical ailment, a psychological reaction, or something else entirely? We may never know, but the tale endures as a chilling reminder of the human mind's mysterious depths—and the strange ways history dances to its own tune.

# THE TUNGUSKA MYSTERY: SIBERIA'S GREAT BLAST

On the morning of June 30, 1908, a remote region of Siberia near the Tunguska River was rocked by an explosion so massive it flattened 80 million trees across 800 square miles. The blast was equivalent to 10-15 megatons of TNT—about 1,000 times the power of the atomic bomb dropped on Hiroshima. Yet, no impact crater was ever found, and the event remains one of the greatest scientific mysteries of the 20th century.

Eyewitnesses described a fireball streaking across the sky, followed by a deafening boom and a shockwave that knocked people off their feet hundreds of miles away. Windows shattered, and the ground trembled as far as Europe. Curiously, despite the devastation, there were no confirmed human casualties due to the sparsely populated area.

Scientists quickly dismissed early theories involving volcanic eruptions or man-made explosives. The prevailing explanation is that a meteor or comet exploded in Earth's atmosphere, releasing its energy mid-air in what's known as an "airburst." The lack of an impact crater supports this theory, though no definitive fragments of the object have been recovered.

More outlandish theories have also surfaced over the years, ranging from alien spacecraft exploding to Nikola Tesla's experimental death ray. While these ideas add to the allure of the Tunguska Event, they remain firmly in the realm of speculation.

To this day, the Tunguska explosion serves as a sobering reminder of the potential hazards lurking in space—and a tantalizing mystery that continues to captivate scientists and storytellers alike.

# THE GHOST SHIP MARY CELESTE

On December 5, 1872, the British brigantine Dei Gratia came across an eerie sight in the Atlantic Ocean: the Mary Celeste, an American merchant ship, drifting aimlessly. Her sails were set, her cargo of alcohol was intact, and there were no signs of distress. Yet, her crew of 10—including the captain, his wife, and their two-year-old daughter—had vanished without a trace.

The ship's log revealed no hints of trouble, with the last entry made on November 25, 1872. The vessel showed no signs of piracy or foul play, and personal belongings were untouched. The only clue was a missing lifeboat, suggesting the crew abandoned ship—but why?

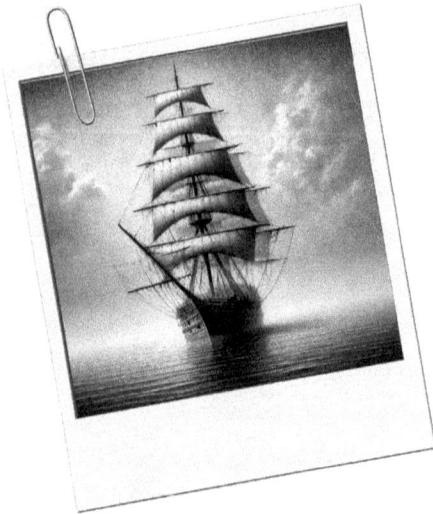

Theories abound. Some suggest an onboard explosion caused by alcohol vapors, leading the crew to panic and evacuate. Others propose a sudden storm or a waterspout frightened them into abandoning the ship. More outlandish ideas involve sea monsters, alien abductions, or even mutiny. However, none of these theories explain why experienced sailors would leave a seaworthy ship.

The mystery deepened when rumors of curses and paranormal activity began to circulate, earning the Mary Celeste her reputation as a ghost ship. Fictionalized accounts, including an embellished story by Arthur Conan Doyle, only added to the legend.

Despite countless investigations, the fate of the Mary Celeste's crew remains unknown. Over 150 years later, the ship's silent journey through the Atlantic continues to fascinate and baffle, a haunting tale of the sea's vast and unyielding mysteries.

# BLACKBEARD'S FINAL STAND

The notorious pirate Blackbeard, born Edward Teach, ruled the seas during the early 18th century's Golden Age of Piracy. With his menacing appearance—complete with a thick black beard and lit fuses in his hat to create a terrifying aura of smoke—he became one of the most feared figures in maritime history. But even the most infamous pirate couldn't escape justice forever.

In November 1718, Blackbeard met his end in a dramatic battle off the coast of North Carolina. After terrorizing the American colonies and blockading ports, he had drawn the ire of Virginia Governor Alexander Spotswood, who sent British naval forces to capture or kill him. Led by Lieutenant Robert Maynard, two ships, the Ranger and the Jane, were

dispatched to confront the pirate and his crew.

Blackbeard's ship, the Queen Anne's Revenge, had already run aground earlier that year, forcing him to use a smaller vessel, Adventure. Maynard caught up to him near Ocracoke Island. Despite being outnumbered, Blackbeard didn't go down without a fight. He and his crew fiercely battled the British, and legend has it that Blackbeard was shot five times and stabbed over 20 times before succumbing.

After the battle, Maynard displayed Blackbeard's severed head on the bow of his ship as a warning to other pirates. The gruesome trophy marked the end of one of history's most infamous marauders.

Blackbeard's death signaled the decline of the pirate era, but his legend lives on, immortalized in tales of buried treasure, ghostly appearances, and his larger-than-life persona. To this day, the name Blackbeard evokes images of daring exploits and the untamed freedom of the high seas.

# THE MAN WHO SOLD THE EIFFEL TOWER — TWICE

Victor Lustig, a name synonymous with audacious scams, pulled off one of the most brazen cons in history—not once, but twice—by "selling" the Eiffel Tower. Born in 1890 in Austria-Hungary, Lustig was a master of deception, fluent in multiple languages, and skilled at exploiting the greed of others.

In 1925, Lustig read a newspaper article about the Eiffel Tower's high maintenance costs, sparking his infamous scheme. Posing as a government official, he invited scrap metal dealers to a luxurious Parisian hotel under the pretense that the city planned to dismantle the tower. He presented forged documents, emphasizing the need for secrecy to avoid public outcry. His performance

was so convincing that one dealer, André Poisson, handed over a large sum to secure the "deal." Lustig fled to Austria with the money before the scam was discovered.

Amazingly, Lustig returned to Paris a few months later and repeated the con with another group of dealers. This time, however, his intended victim grew suspicious and contacted the police, forcing Lustig to flee before the transaction could be completed.

Lustig's audacity didn't end there. He later moved to the United States, where he swindled millions through counterfeit bonds and even conned the infamous gangster Al Capone out of $5,000 — only to return the money, earning Capone's trust for future schemes.

Victor Lustig was eventually arrested in 1935 and spent the rest of his life in Alcatraz. Yet, his "sale" of the Eiffel Tower remains one of the greatest cons of all time, a testament to the power of confidence and cunning over common sense.

# THE GREAT MOLASSES FLOOD
## OF 1919

On a chilly January afternoon in 1919, Boston's North End was transformed into a scene of chaos and destruction when a massive wave of molasses swept through the streets. A giant storage tank owned by the Purity Distilling Company had burst, releasing over 2 million gallons of sticky, brown syrup at speeds of up to 35 miles per hour.

The wave, standing 25 feet high at its peak, destroyed buildings, overturned vehicles, and carried debris in its path. Tragically, 21 people lost their lives, and more than 150 were injured. Horses, unable to escape the viscous flood, became stuck and perished, and the smell of molasses lingered in the city for months.

The tank had shown signs of weakness long before the disaster, with workers reporting leaks and strange groaning noises. However, the company ignored these warnings, painting the tank brown to hide the leaks and brushing off concerns from residents.

The aftermath of the flood saw a lengthy legal battle, as victims and their families sued the company. The investigation revealed that the tank had been hastily constructed with substandard materials, and Purity Distilling was ultimately found liable. The case set a precedent for corporate accountability, leading to stricter regulations for industrial structures.

The Great Molasses Flood remains a bizarre yet sobering reminder of the consequences of negligence. To this day, Bostonians refer to it as "The Boston Molassacre," a darkly humorous name for one of the city's most unusual tragedies.

# THE CURSE OF THE HOPE DIAMOND

T he Hope Diamond, a stunning 45.52-carat blue gem, is one of the most famous jewels in the world—but it's also surrounded by tales of misfortune and tragedy. Over the centuries, the diamond's owners have suffered mysterious deaths, financial ruin, and public disgrace, leading many to believe it is cursed.

The story begins in the 17th century when a French merchant, Jean-Baptiste Tavernier, acquired the diamond in India. According to legend, the gem was stolen from a sacred statue of a Hindu goddess, invoking a curse on anyone who possessed it. Tavernier later died in poverty, and his body was reportedly ravaged by wolves—a grue-

some end that fueled the curse's mythos.

The diamond eventually made its way to King Louis XIV of France, who had it cut and renamed the "French Blue." It became part of the royal treasury, but its presence did not prevent misfortune. Louis XVI and Marie Antoinette, who wore the diamond, were famously executed during the French Revolution. The diamond disappeared during the upheaval, only to resurface years later in London, recut into its current form.

In the 20th century, the gem passed through the hands of several wealthy owners, each facing their own troubles. Socialite Evelyn Walsh McLean, who purchased the diamond in 1911, endured a series of personal tragedies, including the loss of her son and daughter, and the financial collapse of her family.

Today, the Hope Diamond resides safely in the Smithsonian Institution, where millions of visitors marvel at its beauty. Whether the curse is real or simply a series of unfortunate coincidences, the legend ensures the diamond's story is as captivating as the gem itself.

# THE LEGEND OF THE GREEN CHILDREN OF WOOLPIT

In 12th-century England, a peculiar tale emerged from the small village of Woolpit, Suffolk, that continues to baffle historians and folklorists alike. Two children—a boy and a girl—were found near a wolf trap, dressed in unfamiliar clothing, speaking an unknown language, and most curiously, their skin was green.

The villagers took the children in, but they initially refused all food except for raw beans. Over time, their diets expanded, and their green hue gradually faded. As the children learned English, they shared a story that only deepened the mystery. They claimed to have come from a land called St. Martin's Land, a place of perpetual twilight

where everyone had green skin. They said they were tending their family's livestock when they heard a strange sound and suddenly found themselves in Woolpit.

Sadly, the boy fell ill and died shortly after their discovery, but the girl thrived, eventually integrating into the community and marrying. She provided no further explanation for their origins, leaving the villagers—and later historians—to speculate.

Some researchers suggest the children may have been Flemish orphans displaced by war, their odd appearance possibly caused by malnutrition. Others believe the story is rooted in medieval folklore, symbolizing themes of otherworldliness or spiritual transformation. And of course, there are those who see it as evidence of extraterrestrial or interdimensional beings.

Whatever the truth, the legend of the Green Children of Woolpit endures as one of England's most enchanting and enigmatic tales, leaving us to wonder: were they merely lost children, or visitors from another world?

# THE MYSTERY OF OAK ISLAND'S MONEY PIT

For over 200 years, treasure hunters have been captivated by the enigmatic Money Pit on Oak Island, a small island off the coast of Nova Scotia, Canada. The legend began in 1795 when a young boy named Daniel McGinnis discovered a mysterious depression in the ground. Convinced it was a buried treasure site, he and his friends began digging, uncovering layers of wooden planks every ten feet—a clear sign that the pit had been engineered.

As word spread, professional treasure hunters joined the quest. Over the decades, searchers uncovered tantalizing clues, including stone inscriptions, strange artifacts, and evidence of booby traps designed to flood the pit. One inscribed stone reportedly read, "Forty feet below, two million pounds are buried." Yet, despite countless efforts, no treasure has been definitively recovered.

Theories about what lies at the bottom of the Money Pit range from pirate treasure, such as Captain Kidd's hoard, to lost religious relics like the Ark of the Covenant or Shakespearean manuscripts. Some believe the pit was constructed by the Knights Templar to protect their secrets, while skeptics argue it's merely a natural sinkhole.

The search has been perilous. At least six people have died in pursuit of the treasure, fueling a local superstition that the pit will only yield its secrets after seven lives have been lost.

Today, Oak Island remains a hotspot for treasure hunters and curious visitors. Whether the Money Pit is a genuine trove or an elaborate hoax, its enduring allure lies in the mystery—a riddle buried deep in the heart of history.

# THE DYATLOV PASS: A CHILLING RUSSIAN MYSTERY

In January 1959, nine experienced hikers set out on a trek into the Ural Mountains in Soviet Russia. Led by Igor Dyatlov, the group was well-prepared for the harsh conditions. But on the night of February 1, something went terribly wrong. Days later, rescuers found their campsite in disarray: the hikers' tent was slashed open from the inside, and their bodies were scattered across the snowy landscape under bizarre circumstances.

Some hikers were found shoeless and barely dressed, as if they had fled in a panic. Others bore horrific injuries — one had a fractured skull, and two had chest fractures so severe they were compared to a car crash. Yet, there were no external wounds. Even stranger, one victim's body showed traces of radiation, and their skin appeared unusually tan.

Theories about what caused the tragedy have run wild. Some suggest an avalanche forced the hikers to cut their way out of the tent, but the site showed no evidence of one. Others point to infrasound, a rare phenomenon that can induce panic and disorientation. More sensational ideas include secret military experiments, encounters with a Yeti, or even alien abduction.

In 2019, Russian authorities reopened the case and attributed the deaths to a "slab avalanche," a sudden collapse of snow. However, this explanation has not satisfied skeptics, as it fails to account for the radiation or the peculiar injuries.

The Dyatlov Pass Incident remains an unsolved enigma, capturing imaginations worldwide. It's a chilling reminder of nature's power—and the mysteries it still holds.

# THE MAN WHO LIVED
# WITHOUT A HEARTBEAT

In 2011, Craig Lewis, a 55-year-old man from Texas, became the first person in history to live without a pulse. Diagnosed with amyloidosis, a rare condition where abnormal proteins build up in organs, Lewis's heart was failing rapidly. Traditional treatments, including a heart transplant, were not an option. Facing imminent death, his doctors proposed a radical solution: replacing his heart with a device that would circulate blood without creating a heartbeat.

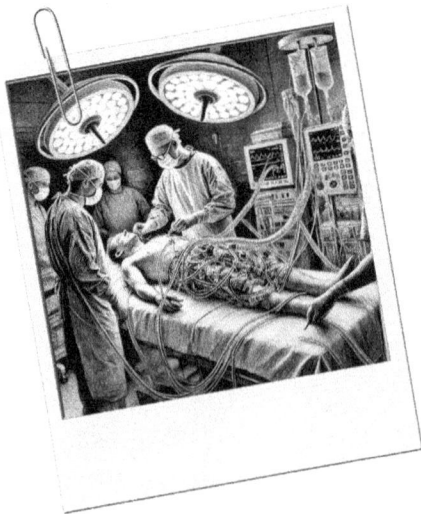

Drs. Billy Cohn and Bud Frazier from the Texas Heart Institute designed the groundbreaking device, which used continuous flow technology to pump blood through the body. Unlike traditional artificial hearts, this device didn't mimic the rhythmic beating of a heart but instead maintained a steady flow of blood.

In a high-stakes surgery, Lewis's heart was removed and replaced with the device. When the operation was complete, he had no pulse. Yet, astonishingly, he was alive, conscious, and able to interact with his family.

The procedure sparked widespread amazement and philosophical questions. Could someone be considered alive without a heartbeat, the very symbol of life itself? The answer, in Lewis's case, was a resounding yes.

Although Lewis passed away five weeks later due to complications from his underlying disease, his story marked a significant milestone in medical science. The success of the device opened new possibilities for treating heart failure and redefined what it means to live.

Craig Lewis's legacy lives on as a testament to human ingenuity, courage, and the power of medical innovation to challenge our understanding of life itself.

# MOUNT TAMBORA: THE ERUPTION THAT SHOOK HISTORY

I n April 1815, Mount Tambora, a volcano on the Indonesian island of Sumbawa, erupted with such ferocity that it became the largest volcanic eruption in recorded history. The explosion was so massive that it could be heard over 1,200 miles away, and the ash plume reached a staggering 28 miles into the sky. The eruption ejected an estimated 36 cubic miles of material, burying entire villages and killing tens of thousands of people.

The immediate devastation was catastrophic, but the long-term effects were even more far-reaching. Ash and sulfur dioxide particles spewed into the atmosphere, blocking sunlight and disrupting global weather patterns. 1816 became known as "The Year Without a Summer." Temperatures plummeted, crops failed, and famine swept across Europe, Asia, and North America. It is estimated that over 100,000 additional deaths worldwide were caused by the resulting food shortages and disease outbreaks.

The bizarre weather inspired cultural and scientific milestones. In Switzerland, Mary Shelley and her companions, trapped indoors by the relentless cold and rain, penned ghost stories. Shelley's contribution was *Frankenstein*, a novel born from the eerie atmosphere of Tambora's aftermath. Meanwhile, the darkened skies led to advancements in the study of meteorology and volcanic activity.

Mount Tambora's eruption serves as a stark reminder of nature's immense power to shape human history. Its impact stretched far beyond its fiery explosion, affecting lives, art, and science in ways that continue to resonate today.

# THE UNBREAKABLE GLASS OF PRINCE RUPERT'S DROPS

In the 17th century, a seemingly magical glass invention captivated the scientific world: Prince Rupert's Drops. These teardrop-shaped glass objects, formed by dripping molten glass into cold water, exhibited an incredible paradox—they were virtually unbreakable at their bulbous ends but could shatter explosively with the slightest pressure at their tails.

Named after Prince Rupert of the Rhine, who introduced them to England, these drops became a source of fascination and experimentation. Their unique properties baffled scientists for centuries. The bulbous head of the drop could withstand hammer blows, while a single nick to the tail could cause the entire structure to dis-

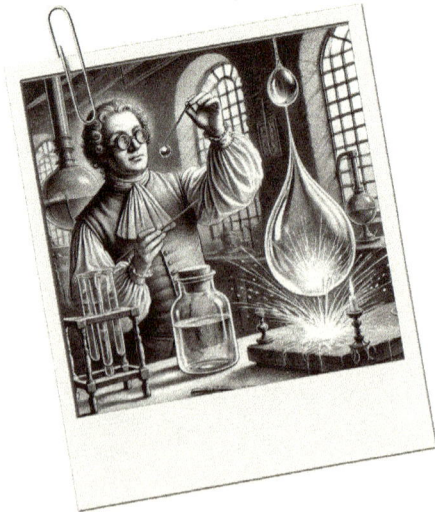

integrate instantly into fine powder.

The secret lies in the rapid cooling process. When molten glass is plunged into water, the exterior cools and solidifies almost immediately, while the interior contracts as it cools more slowly. This creates immense compressive stress on the surface and tensile stress inside. The balance of these forces makes the head incredibly strong but leaves the tail critically weak.

Prince Rupert's Drops became an early tool for studying material strength and stress distribution. Their explosive nature also made them a favorite party trick among royals and scientists, delighting audiences with their dramatic shattering.

Today, these drops remain a staple in physics demonstrations, showcasing the interplay between material science and curiosity. Prince Rupert's Drops remind us that even the simplest experiments can reveal astonishing complexities in the world around us.

# THE STANLEY HOTEL: THE HAUNTING THAT NEVER LEFT

Nestled in the mountains of Estes Park, Colorado, the Stanley Hotel is a picturesque retreat with stunning views and historic charm. But beneath its elegant façade lies a reputation that has made it one of the most famous haunted locations in America.

The hotel was built in 1909 by inventor Freelan Oscar Stanley, who sought a cure for his tuberculosis in the crisp mountain air. Though Stanley recovered, his hotel gained notoriety not for its luxury, but for its spectral residents. Guests and staff have reported eerie occurrences for decades, from phantom footsteps and disembodied laughter to objects moving on their own.

One of the most active areas is Room 217, where housekeeper Elizabeth Wilson was injured in a gas explosion in 1911. She survived and reportedly stayed loyal to her post—even in death. Guests have claimed to see her ghost tidying the room or unpacking their clothes.

The Stanley Hotel's haunting legacy reached new heights when author Stephen King stayed there in 1974. During his visit, he experienced vivid dreams and an overwhelming sense of unease, which inspired his iconic horror novel *The Shining*. While the hotel wasn't used in the film adaptation, it remains closely tied to the story and has embraced its spooky reputation, offering ghost tours and paranormal investigations.

Whether you're a skeptic or a believer, the Stanley Hotel continues to captivate visitors with its mysterious allure. It's a place where history and the supernatural collide, inviting you to check in—but perhaps not to check out.

# THE MIRACLE OF THE DANCING FOREST

D eep within Russia's Kaliningrad region lies an enigmatic natural wonder known as the Dancing Forest. This peculiar woodland, part of the Curonian Spit National Park, is famous for its oddly shaped pine trees. Instead of growing straight and tall, these trees twist, spiral, and curve into loops, resembling a surreal dance frozen in time.

Planted in the 1960s as part of a reforestation project, the trees' strange formations have puzzled scientists and sparked local legends. Some believe the forest is enchanted, claiming that the trees' contortions are the result of mystical energy flows or supernatural forces. Others see it as a spiritual place, where visitors can

recharge their energy or make a wish by walking through the loops.

Scientific explanations, however, suggest a more mundane cause. One theory is that strong winds and unstable sandy soil influenced the trees' growth patterns. Another posits that a particular type of caterpillar damaged the young saplings, causing them to grow in unusual directions. Yet, no definitive explanation has been confirmed, leaving the Dancing Forest a mystery.

The site has become a popular destination for tourists and photographers, who marvel at its otherworldly beauty. Walking among the twisted trunks, it's easy to feel a sense of wonder and curiosity about the forces—natural or otherwise—that shaped this captivating landscape.

Whether a product of nature, chance, or legend, the Dancing Forest stands as a testament to the world's strange and enduring mysteries, inviting us to explore its secrets one winding path at a time.

# THE MYSTERY OF THE MOVING STONES

In the heart of California's Death Valley lies Racetrack Playa, a desolate, dry lakebed surrounded by rugged mountains. Here, one of nature's most peculiar phenomena unfolds: rocks, some weighing hundreds of pounds, appear to move across the flat surface, leaving long, winding trails behind them. For decades, these "sailing stones" baffled scientists and visitors alike.

The trails are unmistakable, often stretching for dozens of feet in seemingly random patterns. What's more puzzling is that no one had ever witnessed the stones in motion, leading to wild theories. Some speculated about magnetic forces or underground vibrations. Others at-

tributed the movement to extraterrestrial intervention or supernatural activity.

In 2014, researchers finally solved the mystery. Using GPS trackers and time-lapse photography, they discovered that a combination of natural elements was responsible. During winter nights, a thin layer of water collects on the lakebed and freezes into sheets of ice. As the sun rises, the ice begins to crack and melt, creating floating panels that are pushed by light winds. These panels nudge the stones along the slippery surface, leaving trails in the soft mud beneath.

While the explanation may seem mundane, the spectacle remains extraordinary. The stones' slow, silent journeys remind us of nature's ability to surprise and intrigue us with its ingenuity.

Even with the mystery solved, Racetrack Playa continues to draw curious visitors, eager to see the enigmatic rocks and their graceful trails. It's a testament to the beauty of the unexplained—and the joy of uncovering its secrets.

# ROANOKE COLONY: THE LOST CITY MYSTERY

In 1587, a group of English settlers, led by Governor John White, arrived on Roanoke Island, off the coast of present-day North Carolina, to establish a new colony. The settlement, known as Roanoke, was intended to be England's first permanent foothold in the New World. But when White returned from a supply trip to England in 1590, he found the colony abandoned, its 115 inhabitants gone without a trace.

The only clue left behind was the word "CROAT-OAN" carved into a wooden post and "CRO" etched into a nearby tree. The colonists' houses had been dismantled, not destroyed, suggesting an organized departure rather than a violent attack. White took the carvings as a

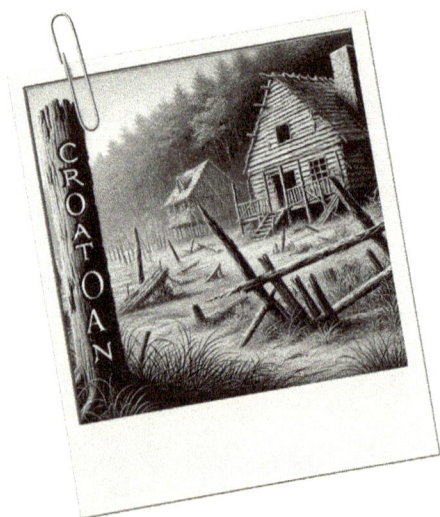

sign that the settlers had relocated to Croatoan Island (now Hatteras Island), but bad weather and dwindling resources prevented him from searching further.

The mystery of the "Lost Colony" has persisted for centuries, giving rise to numerous theories. Some suggest the settlers integrated with local Native American tribes, while others believe they succumbed to disease, starvation, or attacks from hostile tribes. More speculative ideas propose that they fell victim to Spanish raiders or even supernatural forces.

Archaeological digs in recent years have uncovered artifacts on Hatteras Island and mainland sites that may be linked to the colonists, but no definitive evidence has been found. The fate of the Roanoke settlers remains one of America's oldest and most enduring mysteries.

The tale of Roanoke continues to capture imaginations, symbolizing both the hope and peril of early colonization. It's a haunting reminder of the fragility of human endeavors—and the secrets that history keeps hidden.

# THE MAN WHO SURVIVED
# TWO ATOMIC BOMBS

Tsutomu Yamaguchi, a Japanese engineer, holds the harrowing distinction of being one of the few people to survive both atomic bombings during World War II—an ordeal so extraordinary it almost defies belief.

On August 6, 1945, Yamaguchi was in Hiroshima on a business trip when the first atomic bomb, "Little Boy," detonated. He was about two miles from ground zero, yet the blast threw him into the air, ruptured his eardrums, and burned much of his upper body. Despite his injuries, he managed to make his way to an air-raid shelter and spent the night there, surrounded by devastation.

The next day,

Yamaguchi began his journey home to Nagasaki, over 180 miles away. On August 9, as he was recounting his Hiroshima experience to colleagues at work, the second atomic bomb, "Fat Man," exploded over Nagasaki. Once again, Yamaguchi was about two miles from the epicenter. Though suffering additional injuries, he miraculously survived a second time.

Yamaguchi lost many friends and family members in the bombings, and he endured long-term health issues from radiation exposure. However, he lived a full life, passing away in 2010 at the age of 93. In his later years, he became an outspoken advocate for nuclear disarmament, sharing his story to promote peace and prevent future use of atomic weapons.

Tsutomu Yamaguchi's survival is a remarkable testament to human resilience amid unimaginable horror. His life serves as both a sobering reminder of war's devastating power and a powerful call for a world without nuclear weapons.

# THE LIBRARY OF ALEXANDRIA: A LOST LEGACY

The Library of Alexandria, one of the most renowned centers of learning in the ancient world, has become a symbol of human curiosity and intellectual ambition. Built in the Egyptian city of Alexandria during the reign of Pharaoh Ptolemy II in the 3rd century BCE, the library aimed to collect all the world's knowledge under one roof. It's said that its shelves held hundreds of thousands of scrolls, covering topics from astronomy and mathematics to medicine and philosophy.

The library attracted scholars from across the Mediterranean, including some of the greatest minds of the time, such as Euclid and Archimedes. It wasn't just a repository of texts; it was a hub of intellectual collaboration, where thinkers could debate, study, and expand the boundaries of knowledge.

Yet, despite its significance, the Library of Alexandria is remembered as much for its mysterious destruction as for its accomplishments. Over the centuries, it suffered multiple calamities. One theory blames Julius Caesar's siege of Alexandria in 48 BCE, during which a fire consumed parts of the city. Others suggest later rulers, such as Emperor Theophilus or invading Muslim forces, played roles in its demise. Some historians argue that the library declined gradually, its treasures lost to neglect rather than a single catastrophic event.

The loss of the Library of Alexandria is often romanticized as a tragic setback for humanity, with the destruction of countless texts representing the loss of irreplaceable knowledge. While the full scope of its contents remains unknown, the library endures as a symbol of the pursuit of knowledge and the fragility of even the greatest human achievements.

The story of the Library of Alexandria reminds us of the importance of preserving knowledge for future generations and the power of intellectual curiosity to shape our world.

# THE VOYNICH MANUSCRIPT: HISTORY'S GREATEST PUZZLE

The Voynich Manuscript, a 240-page book filled with bizarre illustrations and indecipherable text, has baffled scholars, cryptographers, and linguists for over a century. Discovered in 1912 by rare book dealer Wilfrid Voynich, the manuscript is believed to date back to the early 15th century, though its origins remain shrouded in mystery.

The text is written in an unknown script, with a vocabulary unlike any known language. Its pages are adorned with strange drawings of unrecognizable plants, celestial charts, and naked women in interconnected bathtubs. Some sections resemble alchemical or medical texts, while others seem to detail astronomical

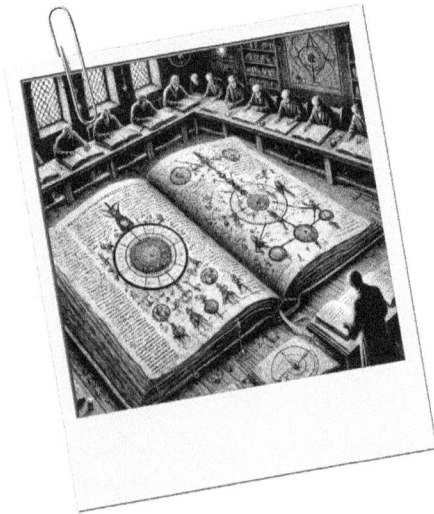

or botanical concepts. Despite countless attempts, no one has been able to conclusively decode its meaning or purpose.

Over the years, theories about the manuscript's origins have ranged from the plausible to the fantastical. Some believe it is a medieval medical guide, while others suspect it was created as an elaborate hoax. More speculative ideas suggest it is a coded text meant to hide secret knowledge, the work of a genius inventor, or even evidence of alien contact.

Advanced studies, including carbon dating, have confirmed the manuscript's age, ruling out a modern forgery. However, its true authorship remains unknown, with names like Roger Bacon, Leonardo da Vinci, and even an anonymous nun being floated as possibilities.

Housed today at Yale University's Beinecke Rare Book & Manuscript Library, the Voynich Manuscript continues to fascinate researchers and enthusiasts alike. Its enigmatic pages serve as a tantalizing reminder of humanity's love for puzzles and the allure of the unknown. Whether a genuine artifact of lost knowledge or a masterful riddle, the Voynich Manuscript ensures its secrets remain just out of reach.

# THE CURSE OF KING TUT'S TOMB

When British archaeologist Howard Carter uncovered the tomb of Pharaoh Tutankhamun in 1922, the world was captivated by the dazzling treasures and the incredible preservation of the boy king's burial site. However, the discovery also gave rise to one of history's most enduring legends: the Curse of King Tut's Tomb.

The curse supposedly promised misfortune to anyone who dared to disturb the pharaoh's eternal rest. Shortly after the tomb's opening, strange and tragic events seemed to lend credence to the myth. The first victim was Lord Carnarvon, the expedition's financial backer, who died from an infected mosquito bite mere

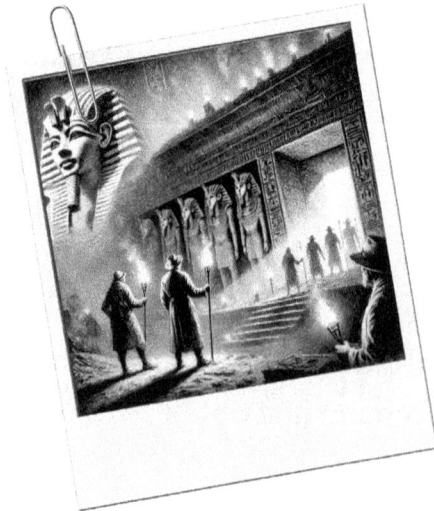

months after entering the tomb. On the day of his death, a power outage plunged Cairo into darkness, and, according to legend, his dog howled and died at the same moment thousands of miles away in England.

Over the years, several others associated with the excavation met untimely ends, fueling rumors of a supernatural curse. These included sudden illnesses, accidents, and mysterious deaths. Newspapers eagerly sensationalized the story, turning it into a global phenomenon.

Skeptics argue that the curse was a product of coincidence and media hype. Many members of the excavation team, including Carter himself, lived long and uneventful lives. Furthermore, the tomb's walls bore no inscriptions warning of a curse, and scientific explanations, such as exposure to ancient mold or bacteria, have been suggested for the illnesses.

Despite the doubts, the legend of King Tut's curse remains irresistible. It adds an air of mystery and danger to one of archaeology's greatest discoveries, reminding us of the allure—and the fear—of unlocking the secrets of the past.

# THE MAN WHO CHEATED DEATH: FRANE SELAK

Frane Selak, a music teacher from Croatia, has earned the nickname "the world's luckiest unlucky man" due to a string of near-death experiences that defy all odds. Over the course of his life, Selak survived seven freak accidents that could have easily claimed his life, leaving him as a living legend of extraordinary fortune.

His brush with death began in 1962 when a train he was riding derailed into an icy river, killing 17 passengers. Selak managed to swim to safety with only a broken arm. A year later, he was on his first and only airplane flight when a door malfunction caused him to be ejected mid-air. Miraculously, he landed in a haystack and

walked away with minor injuries.

Over the next few decades, Selak survived a bus crash into a river, multiple car explosions, and being hit by a city bus. In one incident, his car skidded off a mountain road, and he leaped out just before it plunged into a gorge. Each time, he emerged alive and relatively unscathed, cementing his reputation as a man who could not be killed.

In 2003, Selak's improbable luck took a more positive turn when he won the lottery, pocketing nearly $1 million. He used his winnings to buy a house for his family and live a quiet life, eventually giving much of his fortune away, claiming that money wasn't the key to happiness.

Frane Selak's life is a testament to resilience and the unpredictability of fate. Whether you see his story as luck, destiny, or sheer improbability, it's hard not to marvel at the man who seemingly cheated death time and time again.

# THE STATUE THAT CRIED BLOOD

In 1973, a small church in the Italian town of Civitavecchia became the center of a modern-day miracle—or controversy—when a statue of the Virgin Mary reportedly began to cry blood. The statue, a modest gift from a local artist, stood quietly in the church for years before the first strange occurrence. Witnesses claimed to see red streaks, resembling tears, flowing from the statue's eyes.

Word spread quickly, and pilgrims flocked to

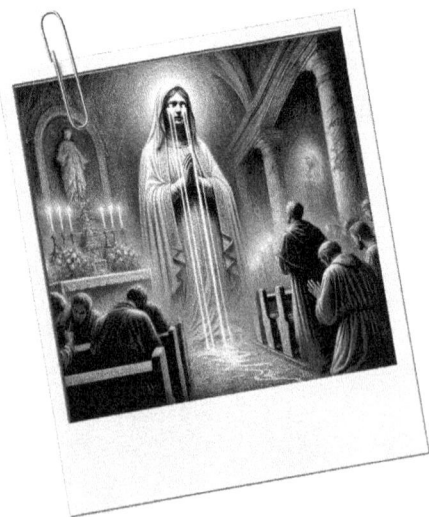

the church, hoping to witness the phenomenon themselves. Many believed it was a sign from heaven, a call for repentance, or a warning of impending disaster. The faithful knelt in prayer, while skeptics questioned whether the "tears" were a clever hoax.

The Catholic Church launched an investigation, collecting samples of the blood-like substance. Tests revealed that the substance was human blood, further fueling speculation and debate. However, the source of the blood—and how it appeared on the statue—remained unexplained.

Over the years, similar occurrences have been reported in other parts of the world, from weeping statues to paintings that exude oil or water. Each case has its share of believers and doubters, sparking debates over faith, science, and the unexplainable.

To this day, the crying Virgin Mary of Civitavecchia remains a mystery. Whether divine intervention, a natural phenomenon, or an elaborate trick, the statue continues to inspire awe and curiosity. It serves as a reminder of humanity's enduring fascination with miracles and the fine line between faith and skepticism.

# THE MYSTERIOUS HUM HEARD AROUND THE WORLD

In cities and towns across the globe, a strange and persistent noise has been baffling residents and scientists for decades. Known simply as "The Hum," this low-frequency sound is often described as a faint, droning noise that can only be heard by certain people. While it has been reported in places like Taos, New Mexico; Bristol, England; and even Largs, Scotland, the exact cause of The Hum remains a mystery.

Those who hear it describe it as maddening, often likening it to the sound of a distant diesel engine or a constant vibration. For some, it's merely an annoyance; for others, it leads to headaches, sleep disturbances, and even psychological distress. What makes The Hum

even more puzzling is that it's not picked up by microphones or audio equipment, suggesting it's either highly localized or not a traditional sound at all.

Over the years, various theories have been proposed. Some scientists suggest industrial machinery, distant traffic, or natural geological phenomena as possible sources. Others speculate that The Hum might be linked to low-frequency electromagnetic waves or even a rare form of tinnitus. A few have ventured into more outlandish territory, attributing it to secret government projects, UFO activity, or extraterrestrial communication.

Despite extensive studies, no definitive explanation has emerged. The Hum seems to appear and vanish without warning, leaving communities perplexed and researchers stumped. For now, it remains an unsolved enigma—a haunting reminder of how much we still don't understand about the world around us.

Whether a natural phenomenon or something far stranger, The Hum continues to intrigue and unsettle those who hear it, a sound that lingers in both the ears and the imagination.

# THE LEGEND OF EL DORADO: THE LOST CITY OF GOLD

For centuries, explorers and adventurers have been captivated by the legend of El Dorado, a mythical city of gold hidden deep within South America. The tale originated from indigenous stories about a Muisca tribal ceremony in present-day Colombia, where a chieftain was said to cover himself in gold dust and dive into Lake Guatavita as an offering to the gods.

When Spanish conquistadors arrived in the Americas in the 16th century, they heard tales of this "Golden Man" and the riches of his people. Over time, the story evolved into the idea of an entire city made of gold, hidden in the jungle and waiting to be discovered. Fueled

by greed and ambition, expeditions set out to find El Dorado, often at great cost. Men like Francisco de Orellana and Sir Walter Raleigh ventured into the Amazon, facing disease, starvation, and hostile terrain, but the city remained elusive.

Lake Guatavita itself became a focal point of the search. In the 16th century, Spanish colonists attempted to drain the lake, uncovering gold artifacts but not the treasure trove they had hoped for. Modern archaeologists have also explored the lake, but the dream of finding a golden city has proven as intangible as ever.

Today, El Dorado is widely regarded as a legend rather than a real location. However, its allure persists, symbolizing humanity's endless quest for wealth, glory, and the unknown. Whether it existed or not, El Dorado continues to inspire stories, art, and the imagination of those who dream of uncovering hidden treasures.

# THE SALEM WITCH TRIALS: A DARK CHAPTER IN HISTORY

In 1692, the small Puritan community of Salem, Massachusetts, was gripped by hysteria that would lead to one of the most infamous episodes of mass panic in American history: the Salem Witch Trials. Over the course of a year, more than 200 people were accused of practicing witchcraft, and 20 were executed—19 by hanging and one, Giles Corey, pressed to death with heavy stones.

The panic began in February when several young girls in Salem Village started exhibiting strange behaviors, including fits, screaming, and contortions. The local doctor, unable to find a medical explanation, declared the cause to be witchcraft. The girls accused three

women: Sarah Good, a beggar; Sarah Osborne, an elderly woman; and Tituba, an enslaved woman from the Caribbean. Under duress, Tituba confessed and claimed that more witches were lurking in the community, igniting a frenzy of accusations.

The trials were marked by dubious evidence, including "spectral testimony," where accusers claimed to see spirits or visions of the accused committing acts of witchcraft. Fear, religious zealotry, and personal vendettas fueled the chaos, with neighbors turning against each other in a desperate bid to prove their innocence.

By September 1692, the hysteria began to wane as doubts about the validity of the accusations grew. Governor William Phips finally put an end to the trials, and many of the convicted were later exonerated. However, the damage was done, leaving a lasting stain on Salem's history.

The Salem Witch Trials stand as a cautionary tale about the dangers of fear, prejudice, and the erosion of due process. Today, Salem draws thousands of visitors who come to learn about this tragic chapter and reflect on the consequences of unchecked mass hysteria.

# THE BIZARRE CASE OF D.B. COOPER

O n November 24, 1971, an ordinary flight from Portland to Seattle became the backdrop for one of the greatest unsolved mysteries in American history. A man known only as "D.B. Cooper" hijacked Northwest Orient Flight 305, claiming he had a bomb in his briefcase. Calm and composed, Cooper handed a note to the flight attendant, demanding $200,000 in cash, four parachutes, and a fuel truck ready to refuel the plane upon landing in Seattle.

Authorities complied with his demands, delivering the ransom and parachutes when the plane landed. Cooper released the passengers and directed the crew to take off again, heading toward Mexico City at a low altitude and slow speed. Somewhere over the dense forests of Washington state, Cooper opened the plane's rear stairway and jumped into the night with the money strapped to his body.

Despite an extensive search, neither Cooper nor his remains were ever found. The FBI scoured the rugged terrain, using helicopters, boats, and ground teams, but the trail went cold. Years later, in 1980, a young boy discovered $5,800 in decayed $20 bills along the Columbia River, matching the serial numbers of the ransom money. However, this clue raised more questions than answers.

Over the decades, numerous theories have emerged. Some believe Cooper died in the jump, while others insist he survived and lived out his life in obscurity. Suspects have ranged from former military paratroopers to career criminals, but no conclusive evidence has ever surfaced.

The case was officially closed in 2016, yet the mystery of D.B. Cooper continues to fascinate. Whether seen as a daring antihero or a reckless criminal, Cooper's story remains one of the most audacious heists in history—and a puzzle that may never be solved.

# THE GHOST SHIP FLYING DUTCHMAN

For centuries, sailors have whispered tales of the Flying Dutchman, a ghostly ship doomed to wander the seas for eternity. Often sighted as a spectral vessel glowing with an eerie light, the Flying Dutchman is said to bring bad luck to those who encounter it—a chilling omen of impending disaster.

The legend traces back to the 17th century and a Dutch captain named Hendrick van der Decken. According to folklore, van der Decken was attempting to navigate the treacherous waters of the Cape of Good Hope when his crew begged him to turn back due to a violent storm. Ignoring their pleas, he swore he would round the cape "even if it took forever." His defiance allegedly

cursed him and his ship to sail the oceans forever, never finding safe harbor.

Over the years, reports of the Flying Dutchman have come from sailors around the world, often under similar circumstances—during storms or foggy weather. One of the most famous sightings was by King George V when he was still a midshipman aboard the HMS Bacchante in 1881. He and several crew members claimed to see a glowing ship off the coast of Australia, only for it to vanish moments later.

While modern explanations point to optical illusions like fata morgana mirages, the legend persists in maritime folklore. The Flying Dutchman has been immortalized in literature, operas, and films, solidifying its place as one of the sea's most haunting mysteries.

Whether a tale of supernatural punishment or a misunderstood natural phenomenon, the Flying Dutchman continues to captivate imaginations, a reminder of the sea's vast and mysterious power.

# THE MYSTERY OF THE BELL WITCH

In the early 19th century, the Bell family of Adams, Tennessee, became the center of one of America's most chilling hauntings, now known as the Bell Witch legend. The tale begins in 1817, when John Bell, a farmer, and his family started experiencing strange phenomena on their property. It began with unusual noises: scratching, knocking, and chains dragging across the floor. Soon, the activity escalated to physical attacks, with members of the family being slapped, pinched, and pushed by an invisible force.

The entity seemed to focus its attention on John Bell and his daughter Betsy. It taunted them with disembodied voices, mocking laughter, and cruel insults. The spirit, which came to be called the

"Bell Witch," also displayed an uncanny intelligence, answering questions and carrying on conversations with visitors. Word of the haunting spread, drawing curious onlookers, including future president Andrew Jackson, who reportedly fled the house after witnessing the spirit's wrath.

The Bell Witch's motives were unclear, but the entity seemed to harbor a particular hatred for John Bell, whom it referred to as "Old Jack." In 1820, after years of torment, John Bell died under mysterious circumstances, with the family finding a vial of unknown liquid near his body. The spirit claimed responsibility for his death, boasting that it had poisoned him.

After John Bell's death, the activity subsided, though occasional reports of strange occurrences persisted. The legend of the Bell Witch has endured, inspiring books, films, and even a tourist industry in Adams, where the Bell Witch Cave remains a popular destination for ghost hunters.

Whether a case of mass hysteria, a clever hoax, or a genuine supernatural event, the Bell Witch legend continues to fascinate and terrify, cementing its place in America's paranormal lore.

# THE STRANGE DISAPPEARANCE OF AGATHA CHRISTIE

On the evening of December 3, 1926, famed mystery novelist Agatha Christie vanished without a trace, sparking a nationwide manhunt and a media frenzy. For 11 days, the "Queen of Crime" became the subject of her very own mystery — one that remains partially unsolved to this day.

Christie's car was discovered abandoned near a chalk quarry in Surrey, England, with an expired driver's license and a fur coat left inside. Police feared the worst, suspecting an accident or foul play. Thousands of volunteers scoured the countryside, and even fellow writers, including Sir Arthur Conan Doyle, joined

the search. Doyle famously took one of Christie's gloves to a medium in hopes of uncovering clues.

The story took a bizarre turn when Christie was found alive and well on December 14 at a luxury hotel in Harrogate, Yorkshire. She had checked in under an assumed name—Theresa Neele, the same surname as her husband's mistress. Despite being recognized by staff and fellow guests, Christie appeared unaware of the uproar surrounding her disappearance.

Christie herself offered no clear explanation, claiming to have suffered from amnesia brought on by emotional stress. At the time, she was dealing with her mother's recent death and the revelation of her husband's affair. While some accepted her account, others suspected it was a deliberate act to embarrass her unfaithful spouse or to escape the pressures of her personal and professional life.

To this day, the true reason for Agatha Christie's disappearance remains a topic of speculation and intrigue. Whether a case of genuine memory loss or a carefully orchestrated stunt, the episode adds another layer of mystery to the life of one of the world's greatest storytellers.

# THE IRON PILLAR OF DELHI: A RUST-PROOF WONDER

Standing in the heart of Qutub Minar Complex in Delhi, India, is an ancient engineering marvel that has puzzled scientists and historians for centuries: the Iron Pillar of Delhi. This 23-foot-tall column, weighing over 13,000 pounds, is made of nearly pure iron yet shows almost no signs of rust, despite being over 1,600 years old and exposed to harsh weather conditions.

The pillar, believed to have been erected during the reign of Chandragupta II in the 4th century CE, is inscribed with Sanskrit text praising the king's military victories. Its remarkable resistance to corrosion has sparked extensive research, with experts suggesting

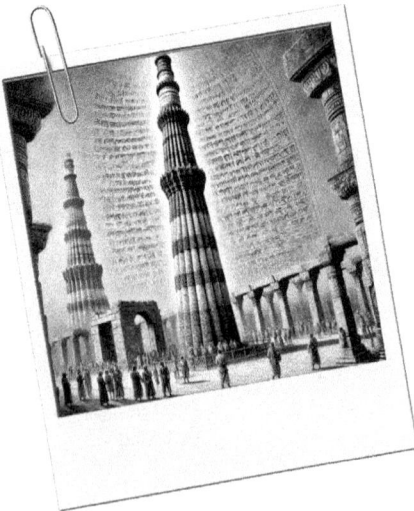

that its composition and construction techniques were far ahead of their time. The iron contains high levels of phosphorus and lacks sulfur and manganese, which together create a protective layer of passive oxide that prevents rusting.

While modern metallurgy can explain the pillar's longevity, its creation remains a testament to the advanced knowledge of ancient Indian blacksmiths. Producing such a massive column with primitive tools and ensuring its durability required exceptional skill and precision.

The Iron Pillar has also become a symbol of cultural and historical pride. Local legend says that anyone who can encircle the pillar with their arms while standing with their back to it will have their wishes granted—a tradition that has left visible marks from centuries of attempts.

Today, the Iron Pillar of Delhi stands as both a historical artifact and a scientific curiosity, reminding us of the ingenuity of ancient civilizations. It's a silent yet powerful testament to human innovation, standing tall against the passage of time.

# THE WOMAN WHO SURVIVED FALLING FROM 33,000 FEET

On January 26, 1972, Vesna Vulović, a 22-year-old flight attendant for JAT Yugoslav Airlines, achieved a grim yet miraculous record: she survived the highest fall without a parachute—33,000 feet. Her story is one of resilience, tragedy, and mystery.

Vulović was aboard Flight 367 en route from Stockholm to Belgrade when an explosion tore through the DC-9 aircraft. The plane disintegrated mid-air, scattering debris and passengers across the snowy mountains of Czechoslovakia. Investigators later determined that a suitcase bomb, allegedly planted by terrorists, caused the explosion.

Amazingly, Vu-

lović was found alive in the wreckage by a local villager. She had been trapped in the plane's tail section, which landed in a thick forest and deep snow, cushioning the impact. Vulović suffered severe injuries, including a fractured skull, three broken vertebrae, and temporary paralysis. She spent months recovering in the hospital, enduring surgeries and intense rehabilitation, but eventually regained her ability to walk.

Her survival defied all odds, earning her a place in the Guinness World Records. Vulović became a national hero in Yugoslavia and an advocate for peace, though she shied away from being labeled a celebrity. "I'm lucky to have survived, and that's enough for me," she often said.

Despite her remarkable story, questions linger about the exact circumstances of the crash, with some conspiracy theories suggesting alternate scenarios. However, Vulović's survival remains a testament to the resilience of the human body and spirit.

Vesna Vulović's incredible fall continues to inspire awe and wonder, reminding us that even in the face of unimaginable odds, survival is possible.

# THE CODEX GIGAS: THE DEVIL'S BIBLE

The Codex Gigas, also known as "The Devil's Bible," is one of the largest and most mysterious manuscripts in the world. Measuring three feet tall and weighing over 165 pounds, the 13th-century book contains 620 pages of Latin text, including the entire Bible, medical knowledge, magical formulas, and a chilling full-page illustration of the devil.

The legend surrounding the Codex Gigas is as dark as its contents. According to folklore, the manuscript was created by a monk in a single night. Condemned to death for breaking his monastic vows, the monk promised to write a book so magnificent it would glorify his order and save his life. When he realized the task was

impossible, he allegedly made a pact with the devil, who completed the manuscript in exchange for the monk's soul. The devil's eerie portrait within the book is said to commemorate this unholy bargain.

Modern scholars dismiss the legend, estimating that it would have taken at least 20 years to complete the Codex Gigas due to its size and meticulous calligraphy. Yet, questions remain about its origins. The manuscript's handwriting is remarkably consistent, suggesting it was written by a single person, and its creation required access to expensive materials, making its provenance a mystery.

Today, the Codex Gigas resides in the National Library of Sweden, where it continues to intrigue visitors with its sheer scale and sinister reputation. Whether a feat of human determination or a relic steeped in myth, the Devil's Bible stands as a reminder of the power—and the peril—of human ambition.

# THE CURSE OF THE PHARAOHS

The Curse of the Pharaohs is one of history's most enduring legends, claiming that anyone who disturbs an ancient Egyptian tomb will face dire consequences. While tales of cursed tombs predate the 20th century, the legend gained global fame after the discovery of King Tutankhamun's tomb in 1922 by British archaeologist Howard Carter.

Soon after the tomb was opened, a series of mysterious deaths fueled rumors of a curse. The most famous victim was Lord Carnarvon, the tomb's financial backer, who died just months after the discovery from an infected mosquito bite. At the moment of his death, it's said that all the lights in Cairo went out, adding an eerie twist to the story. Over the years, other members of the expedition also died prematurely,

further solidifying the curse's reputation.

Scientists and skeptics, however, offer more rational explanations. Some suggest exposure to ancient bacteria, mold, or toxic gases in the tombs could have caused illnesses. Others point to coincidence, noting that Carter himself, who spent years in the tomb, lived until 1939, long after many of his colleagues had passed.

Despite the skepticism, the Curse of the Pharaohs continues to capture imaginations, inspiring movies, books, and even cautious whispers among modern archaeologists. Whether a genuine supernatural force or a product of sensationalist media, the legend serves as a reminder of humanity's fascination with ancient Egypt and the mysteries it still holds.

The Curse of the Pharaohs remains a powerful story of intrigue, danger, and the enduring allure of ancient treasures — an eternal enigma shrouded in gold and shadow.

# THE GREAT LONDON BEER FLOOD

On October 17, 1814, an ordinary day in London's St. Giles district turned into a bizarre disaster when a massive wave of beer swept through the streets. The source of the calamity was the Horse Shoe Brewery, where a 22-foot-tall wooden vat containing over 135,000 gallons of beer suddenly burst. The force of the rupture caused other vats to explode, unleashing a tidal wave of beer estimated at over 323,000 gallons.

The beer flood surged through the densely populated neighborhood, destroying homes, knocking down walls, and even causing part of a nearby tavern to collapse. Tragically, the incident claimed the lives of at least eight people, including women and children, who were unable to escape the deluge.

The disaster became a grim spectacle, drawing crowds of curious onlookers. Some locals reportedly attempted to salvage beer from the streets using buckets and pots, while others simply drank it straight from the flood. The chaos led to a mix of mourning and dark humor, with the event quickly becoming a part of London's folklore.

An investigation later determined that the vat's structural failure was due to poor maintenance, but no one was held accountable. The brewery itself was nearly bankrupted by the incident, though it managed to recover and continue operations for decades.

The Great London Beer Flood remains one of history's most unusual and tragic industrial accidents. It serves as a strange reminder of the fragility of human engineering and the unexpected ways life can turn from mundane to catastrophic in an instant.

# THE MAN IN THE IRON MASK

The mystery of the Man in the Iron Mask has captivated historians and storytellers for centuries. This enigmatic prisoner, held in various French jails during the late 17th century, remains shrouded in intrigue. Most famously, he was confined in the Bastille under the watch of King Louis XIV's trusted jailer, Bénigne Dauvergne de Saint-Mars.

What sets this prisoner apart is the peculiar detail of his imprisonment: his face was always concealed, supposedly by a velvet mask (later popularized as iron in legend). The secrecy surrounding his identity was so strict that guards who spoke of him faced execution. The mystery of who he was—and why his identity needed to be hidden—sparked countless theories.

Some believe he was a disgraced nobleman or military

officer, while others suggest he was a close relative of King Louis XIV, such as an illegitimate half-brother or even a twin. The latter theory, though unsubstantiated, inspired Alexandre Dumas's famous novel *The Man in the Iron Mask*, part of *The Three Musketeers* saga.

Official records from the time offer little clarity. The prisoner died in 1703 and was buried under the name "Marchiali," providing no hints about his origins. Historians have pored over documents, but no definitive answer has emerged, leaving his identity one of France's greatest historical enigmas.

The story of the Man in the Iron Mask endures as a fascinating blend of fact and fiction. Whether a political pawn, a wronged noble, or an innocent victim, his tale reminds us of the enduring power of secrets—and the lengths to which those in power will go to keep them.

# THE MIRACLE OF FLIGHT 571:
# THE ANDES SURVIVORS

On October 13, 1972, Uruguayan Air Force Flight 571, carrying 45 passengers and crew, crashed into the Andes Mountains during a charter flight from Montevideo to Santiago. The passengers, mostly members of a rugby team and their families, faced unimaginable challenges as they struggled to survive in one of the harshest environments on Earth.

The crash left 29 survivors stranded at an altitude

of over 11,000 feet, with freezing temperatures, limited clothing, and only a few days' worth of food. When rescue efforts were called off after ten days, the survivors realized they were on their own. As supplies ran out, they made a grim decision to survive: consuming the bodies of those who had perished in the crash, a choice born of sheer desperation.

Two months later, an avalanche struck their makeshift shelter, killing eight more people. Despite the unrelenting hardships, hope persisted. Two survivors, Nando Parrado and Roberto Canessa, embarked on a daring 10-day trek through the mountains to seek help. Their journey took them across treacherous terrain, with no proper equipment or training, driven only by determination and the will to live.

On December 20, 1972, Parrado and Canessa stumbled upon a Chilean shepherd, who alerted authorities. Rescue teams quickly located the remaining 14 survivors, bringing their 72-day ordeal to an end.

The story of Flight 571 is one of resilience, courage, and the extraordinary lengths humans will go to in the face of adversity. Immortalized in books and films like *Alive*, the tale of the Andes survivors continues to inspire and remind us of the unbreakable human spirit.

# THE MARY TOFT HOAX: THE WOMAN AND THE RABBITS

In 1726, England was gripped by one of the strangest medical hoaxes in history when a woman named Mary Toft claimed she could give birth to rabbits. A poor servant from Godalming, Surrey, Toft's bizarre story began when she allegedly delivered several rabbit parts after a miscarriage. Local doctors, intrigued and baffled, documented her claims and brought her to the attention of prominent physicians.

Toft explained that she had been startled by a rabbit while working in a field during her pregnancy and believed this had caused her body to produce rabbit offspring. Her tale tapped into the 18th-century belief in "maternal impressions," the idea that a pregnant

woman's experiences could physically affect her un-born child.

King George I's personal surgeon, Nathaniel St. André, traveled to examine Toft. Astonishingly, he supported her claims after witnessing her "deliver" rabbit parts. News of the miraculous births spread across England, drawing public fascination and skepticism.

However, the hoax unraveled when Toft was taken to London for further examination. Unable to produce more rabbits under close supervision, she eventually confessed to the scheme. She had been inserting rabbit parts into her body, aided by accomplices, to maintain the ruse. Her motive? Money and fame in a time of poverty and limited opportunities.

The scandal humiliated the medical community, particularly St. André, whose reputation never recovered. Toft was briefly imprisoned but later released, fading into obscurity.

The Mary Toft hoax remains a cautionary tale of gullibility, ambition, and the lengths to which some will go to manipulate belief. It's a story that blends the bizarre with the tragic, leaving us to marvel at one of history's most peculiar deceptions.

# THE MYSTERIOUS DEATH OF EDGAR ALLAN POE

On October 3, 1849, renowned writer Edgar Allan Poe was found delirious and disoriented on the streets of Baltimore, wearing clothes that didn't belong to him. He was taken to Washington College Hospital, where he drifted in and out of consciousness for four days before passing away on October 7. His cause of death was recorded as "congestion of the brain," but no autopsy was performed, leaving his final moments shrouded in mystery.

Poe's strange behavior in his final days only deepened the intrigue. He reportedly called out for someone named "Reynolds" and muttered incoherently. His whereabouts and activities in the days leading up to his discovery remain unknown, fueling speculation about the circumstances of his death.

Over the years, numerous theories have emerged. Some suggest he succumbed to alcohol poisoning, a plausible explanation given his known struggles with drinking. Others propose more sinister causes, such as foul play, rabies, carbon monoxide poisoning, or even a rare brain disease.

One particularly intriguing theory is that Poe was a victim of "cooping," a form of voter fraud common in the 19th century. In this scheme, individuals were kidnapped, drugged or intoxicated, and forced to vote multiple times in disguises—possibly explaining his unfamiliar clothing.

Despite extensive research, no definitive answers have been found, and Poe's death remains one of literary history's greatest unsolved mysteries. His life, filled with darkness and tragedy, ended in a manner as haunting as the tales he wrote.

The enigmatic circumstances of Edgar Allan Poe's death only add to his legacy as a master of the macabre, leaving fans and historians to ponder the fate of one of America's greatest writers.

# ZHENG HE'S VOYAGES: CHINA'S FORGOTTEN EXPLORER

L ong before Columbus set sail for the Americas, a Chinese admiral named Zheng He led some of the most ambitious naval expeditions in history. Between 1405 and 1433, Zheng He commanded seven voyages during the Ming Dynasty, traveling across the Indian Ocean to Southeast Asia, South Asia, the Middle East, and even Africa. His fleet, consisting of hundreds of ships and tens of thousands of men, was unparalleled in size and sophistication.

Zheng He's flagship, known as a treasure ship, was an engineering marvel—over 400 feet long, dwarfing the ships of European explorers. These

vessels carried precious goods, including silk, por-celain, and spices, which Zheng He used to establish trade relations and showcase China's wealth and power. His voyages were not solely about commerce; they were also diplomatic missions, spreading Chinese culture and influence across distant lands.

In his travels, Zheng He visited places like modern-day Sri Lanka, India, and Kenya, bringing back exotic treasures such as giraffes and zebras, which fascinated the Chinese court. However, his expeditions abruptly ended in the 1430s when the Ming government shifted its priorities inward, dismantling the fleet and effectively erasing his legacy.

Zheng He's achievements were largely forgotten in the West until modern historians rediscovered his story. Today, he is celebrated as a pioneer of maritime exploration, his voyages standing as a testament to the advanced seafaring capabilities of 15th-century China.

The voyages of Zheng He remind us that the Age of Exploration was not limited to Europe. His journeys reflect a different era of global exchange and serve as a powerful example of what humanity can achieve when driven by curiosity and ambition.

# THE MYSTERY OF THE ANTIKYTHERA MECHANISM

In 1901, sponge divers off the coast of the Greek island of Antikythera discovered a shipwreck that contained a puzzling artifact now known as the Antikythera Mechanism. Dating back to around 100 BCE, this intricate device is considered the world's first analog computer, designed to predict astronomical events with astonishing precision.

The mechanism consists of a complex system of bronze gears and dials, housed in a wooden box. When turned, it could calculate the positions of the sun, moon, and planets, as well as predict eclipses and track the ancient Greek calendar. The sophistication of its design stunned researchers, as it demonstrated tech-nological knowl-

edge far beyond what was previously thought possible for the era.

For decades, the purpose and construction of the mechanism remained a mystery. Modern imaging techniques, such as X-ray tomography, have revealed its inner workings, shedding light on its advanced engineering. The inscriptions on the device suggest it was used for educational purposes and may have been created by a workshop with ties to renowned Greek scientists like Archimedes or Hipparchus.

Despite these discoveries, many questions remain. How was such an advanced tool created in an era without industrial machinery? Why did this level of technological sophistication seemingly vanish for over a millennium, only to reappear in the Middle Ages? And was the Antikythera Mechanism a one-of-a-kind invention or part of a larger tradition?

The Antikythera Mechanism challenges our understanding of ancient innovation, revealing that the boundaries of human ingenuity often stretch further than we realize. It stands as a testament to the brilliance of ancient minds and the enduring mysteries of history.

# THE GREAT CHICAGO FIRE: FACT AND FOLKLORE

On the evening of October 8, 1871, a fire broke out in a small barn on the southwest side of Chicago. Fueled by dry weather, wooden buildings, and strong winds, the blaze quickly spiraled out of control, engulfing much of the city. By the time it was extinguished two days later, the Great Chicago Fire had destroyed over 17,000 buildings, left 100,000 people homeless, and claimed an estimated 300 lives.

The cause of the fire remains uncertain, but folklore has long pointed to Catherine O'Leary's cow kicking over a lantern in her barn. While this story captured the public imagination, it was likely fabricated by an unscrupulous reporter. In reality, no definitive evidence ever linked

the O'Leary family to the fire, though they endured decades of public blame.

The fire's rapid spread was due to a perfect storm of factors: Chicago's densely packed wooden structures, a lack of modern firefighting equipment, and the city's vulnerability after a prolonged drought. The disaster brought attention to the need for better urban planning and fire safety measures.

In the aftermath, Chicago rose from the ashes, literally and figuratively. The city embraced modern building techniques, including the use of fire-resistant materials like brick and steel. This rebuilding effort transformed Chicago into a hub of architectural innovation, earning it the nickname "The Second City."

The Great Chicago Fire remains a powerful symbol of destruction and resilience. While the cow legend adds a touch of folklore to the story, the real legacy lies in how the city rebuilt, stronger and more determined than ever.

# THE DISAPPEARANCE OF THE SODDER CHILDREN

On Christmas Eve, 1945, a fire engulfed the Sodder family home in Fayetteville, West Virginia. George and Jennie Sodder, along with nine of their ten children, were asleep when the blaze broke out. While four children escaped, the remaining five—Maurice, Martha, Louis, Jennie, and Betty—were presumed dead. However, the mystery surrounding their disappearance has puzzled investigators and captivated the public for decades.

Despite a thorough search of the fire's aftermath, no human remains were ever found, an anomaly considering the intense heat required to completely cremate bones. Additionally, the Sodders reported several strange occurrences before and during the fire. A mysterious phone call, a missing ladder that was later found hidden, and a sabotaged family truck all raised suspicions of foul play.

Over the years, the Sodders became convinced their children had been kidnapped. Sightings of the missing children were reported, and a photo of a young man resembling one of their sons was sent anonymously to the family. A cryptic note on the back read: "Louis Sodder. I love brother Frankie. Ilil boys. A90132 or 35." The Sodders even hired private investigators to follow leads, but the trail always went cold.

The case remains unsolved, with theories ranging from a Mafia vendetta to an elaborate abduction plot. Despite their relentless search, the Sodder family never found definitive answers.

The disappearance of the Sodder children is one of America's most haunting mysteries, blending tragedy and intrigue. It's a tale of a family's unyielding hope, the enduring power of unanswered questions, and a case that continues to perplex and fascinate.

# THE LEGEND OF THE LOCH NESS MONSTER

D eep in the misty waters of Scotland's Loch Ness lies one of the world's most enduring mysteries: the Loch Ness Monster. Affectionately known as "Nessie," this elusive creature has sparked curiosity and debate for centuries, with sightings reported as far back as the 6th century.

The modern legend began in 1933 when a couple claimed to see a massive, dinosaur-like creature crossing the road near the loch. Shortly after, a photograph by Robert Kenneth Wilson, known as the "Surgeon's Photograph," appeared to show a long-necked creature gliding through the water. Though later revealed to be a hoax, the image cemented Nessie's place in popular

culture.

Over the years, countless expeditions have sought to uncover the truth. Sonar scans, underwater cameras, and even DNA studies have been conducted, but none have definitively proven the existence of the monster. Explanations for sightings range from misidentified animals like seals and sturgeons to natural phenomena such as waves and submerged debris.

Despite the lack of concrete evidence, Nessie continues to captivate imaginations worldwide. The Loch Ness Monster has become a symbol of wonder and the unknown, drawing tourists, cryptozoologists, and skeptics alike to the Scottish Highlands.

Whether a real creature, a figment of imagination, or a clever marketing ploy, Nessie's legend endures, reminding us of humanity's love for mystery and the possibility that there's still more to discover in the depths of our world.

# THE MYSTERY OF KASPAR HAUSER

On May 26, 1828, a mysterious teenager appeared in Nuremberg, Germany, sparking one of the most perplexing enigmas of the 19th century. The boy, who called himself Kaspar Hauser, could barely speak or walk and carried a letter addressed to a local military officer. The letter claimed he had been raised in isolation and wished to serve in the army.

When questioned, Hauser's story became even stranger. He claimed to have spent most of his life confined in a dark cell, fed only bread and water, and receiving no human interaction. He knew nothing of the outside world until he was released shortly before arriving in

Nuremberg.

Hauser's sudden appearance and peculiar behavior fascinated the public, and he became an instant sensation. Many speculated that he was of noble descent, possibly the rightful heir to the Grand Duchy of Baden, hidden away to secure another's claim to the throne. Others believed his story was a hoax or that he suffered from a mental illness.

The mystery deepened when, in 1833, Hauser was found with a fatal stab wound. Before dying, he claimed he had been attacked by a stranger who gave him a purse containing a cryptic note. The note's author claimed responsibility for Hauser's upbringing but offered no further explanation. However, inconsistencies in Hauser's account led some to suspect he inflicted the wound himself, possibly as part of a desperate bid for attention.

To this day, the true identity and origin of Kaspar Hauser remain unsolved. Whether a tragic victim or a clever impostor, his story continues to intrigue and mystify, leaving us to ponder the secrets he took to his grave.

# THE VANISHING VILLAGE OF ANJIKUNI LAKE

In the remote wilderness of northern Canada lies one of the strangest and most chilling mysteries in the country's history: the disappearance of an entire Inuit village near Anjikuni Lake. The event, reportedly occurring in 1930, has baffled investigators and inspired eerie tales of the unexplained.

A fur trapper named Joe Labelle, familiar with the region, arrived at the village expecting to find its bustling community. Instead, he found it eerily

deserted. The huts and kayaks were intact, food was left cooking over extinguished fires, and personal belongings were untouched, as if the villagers had vanished in the middle of daily life.

Disturbingly,

Labelle also reported finding the graves of the village's dead emptied, their markers removed, and no signs of where the remains had gone. Even the sled dogs, essential to the villagers' survival, were found dead, frozen and starved, despite an ample food supply left behind.

Labelle alerted the Royal Canadian Mounted Police, who conducted an investigation but found no definitive answers. Theories about the disappearance ranged from starvation and relocation to supernatural forces, alien abduction, or even malevolent spirits from Inuit folklore. However, some skeptics question whether the incident occurred at all, citing a lack of contemporary records.

True or not, the legend of the vanishing village at Anjikuni Lake has endured, becoming a favorite among paranormal enthusiasts. It's a haunting reminder of the vast, uncharted territories of the world and the mysteries they hold, where the line between fact and folklore often blurs.

# THE CURSE OF THE BERMUDA TRIANGLE

The Bermuda Triangle, a loosely defined region between Miami, Bermuda, and Puerto Rico, has gained a reputation as a mysterious zone where ships and planes seemingly vanish without a trace. Over the years, the Triangle has been linked to countless disappearances, earning nicknames like "The Devil's Triangle."

One of the earliest and most famous incidents occurred in 1945 when Flight 19, a group of five U.S. Navy bombers, disappeared during a training mission. The pilots reported compass malfunctions and disorientation before communication was lost. A rescue plane sent to search for them also vanished, fueling the area's

110

sinister reputation. Since then, tales of ghost ships, malfunctioning instruments, and unexplained wreckages have added to the lore.

Theories attempting to explain the Bermuda Triangle range from scientific to fantastical. Natural explanations include magnetic anomalies, methane gas eruptions, rogue waves, and severe weather patterns. Others suggest supernatural causes, such as extraterrestrial activity, time warps, or remnants of the lost city of Atlantis.

Skeptics argue that the Triangle's reputation is exaggerated, pointing out that the number of disappearances is not unusually high for a heavily traveled area. They also highlight the tendency for legends to overshadow mundane explanations like human error and mechanical failure.

Despite these rational arguments, the Bermuda Triangle continues to captivate imaginations. Its enduring mystery symbolizes humanity's fascination with the unknown and serves as a reminder that the ocean, vast and unpredictable, still holds secrets beyond our understanding.

# OPERATION MINCEMEAT: THE MAN WHO WASN'T THERE

D uring World War II, the Allies executed one of history's most ingenious deception plans, codenamed Operation Mincemeat. The mission involved planting false intelligence on a corpse and tricking Nazi Germany into diverting their forces—an audacious strategy that proved remarkably effective.

The plan centered around creating a fictitious identity for the corpse. British intelligence obtained the body of a homeless man who had died of pneumonia and dressed him as "Major William Martin" of the Royal Marines. They loaded him with fake documents suggesting the Allies planned to invade Greece and Sardin-

ia, rather than their true target, Sicily.

In April 1943, a British submarine released the body off the coast of Spain, where it was discovered by local authorities. Knowing that the Spanish government had connections to the Nazis, British agents ensured the documents made their way into German hands.

The deception worked brilliantly. German forces repositioned to defend Greece and Sardinia, leaving Sicily vulnerable. When the Allies launched their invasion of Sicily in July 1943, they encountered far less resistance, marking a pivotal moment in the war.

Operation Mincemeat is remembered as a masterstroke of espionage, combining meticulous planning, creativity, and psychological manipulation. The mission was later immortalized in books and films, cementing its place as one of the most daring and successful military ruses in history.

The story of Operation Mincemeat highlights the power of deception in warfare, where a single, carefully crafted lie can alter the course of history.

# THE MYSTERY OF STONEHENGE

Rising from the Salisbury Plain in England, Stonehenge is one of the world's most iconic and enigmatic monuments. Comprising massive stones arranged in a circular formation, this prehistoric site has puzzled archaeologists and historians for centuries. Who built it, how, and why remain questions that continue to intrigue us.

Construction of Stonehenge began around 3000 BCE and evolved over several millennia. The largest stones, known as sarsens, weigh up to 25 tons each and were transported from over 20 miles away. Even more astonishing, the smaller bluestones came from Wales, some 150 miles distant. The methods used to move these

enormous stones without modern tools or machinery remain a subject of debate.

The purpose of Stonehenge is equally mysterious. Some theories suggest it was a burial site, supported by the discovery of human remains nearby. Others propose it served as an astronomical calendar, aligning with the solstices to mark important seasonal events. Its alignment with celestial bodies suggests a deep understanding of astronomy by its builders.

More speculative ideas link Stonehenge to ancient rituals, Druidic ceremonies, or even extraterrestrial intervention. While these theories capture the imagination, no definitive evidence supports them.

In recent years, advanced archaeological techniques have uncovered new insights, including the discovery of nearby settlements and similar structures. Yet, Stonehenge's full story remains elusive.

This ancient monument stands as a testament to human ingenuity and the enduring allure of the unknown. Stonehenge continues to draw millions of visitors annually, inviting them to marvel at its scale, mystery, and the secrets it still holds.

# THE MIRACLE OF THE SUN: THE FATIMA APPARITIONS

On October 13, 1917, tens of thousands of people gathered in the small Portuguese town of Fatima to witness what would become one of the most famous religious events of the 20th century: the Miracle of the Sun. The phenomenon followed months of reports from three shepherd children—Lucia, Francisco, and Jacinta—who claimed to have seen apparitions of the Virgin Mary.

According to the children, the Virgin Mary had appeared to them multiple times, delivering messages of prayer, repentance, and warnings about global events. She promised a sign on October 13 to convince skeptics of her presence. Word spread, and a massive crowd of be-

lievers, doubters, and journalists gathered in the Cova da Iria field, braving rain and muddy conditions.

What happened next is the subject of intense debate. Witnesses reported seeing the rain suddenly stop, and the clouds part to reveal the sun, which appeared to spin, change colors, and zigzag across the sky. Some described the sun as plummeting toward Earth, causing panic among the crowd. Others claimed their previously soaked clothes were inexplicably dry by the end of the event.

Skeptics attribute the phenomenon to mass hysteria, optical illusions, or meteorological conditions. Scientists argue that staring directly at the sun can cause temporary visual distortions, while others dismiss the event as a hoax or exaggeration. Despite these explanations, many attendees believed they had witnessed a divine miracle.

The Catholic Church later recognized the Fatima apparitions as authentic, and the site became a major pilgrimage destination. The Miracle of the Sun remains a powerful symbol of faith for millions, blending religious devotion with one of history's most enigmatic events.

# THE CURSE OF ÖTZI THE ICEMAN

In 1991, hikers in the Alps near the Austrian-Italian border discovered a remarkably well-preserved mummy encased in ice. Nicknamed Ötzi, the Iceman was determined to be over 5,000 years old, making him one of the oldest and best-preserved mummies ever found. However, alongside the incredible scientific discoveries surrounding Ötzi, a chilling legend began to emerge: the curse of the Iceman.

Since Ötzi's discovery, several individuals connected to him have died under unusual or tragic circumstances. One of the first was forensic pathologist Rainer Henn, who handled Ötzi's body with his bare hands. He died in a car accident en route to a lecture about the Iceman.

Shortly after, mountaineer Kurt Fritz, who helped lead scientists to Ötzi's location, perished in an avalanche. Then, Helmut Simon, one of the hikers who discovered Ötzi, died in a freak blizzard while hiking in the same region.

Over the years, more deaths were attributed to the curse, including that of archaeologist Konrad Spindler, who first studied Ötzi, and journalist Rainer Hölz, who filmed the Iceman's recovery. While many of these deaths can be explained as coincidences, the string of tragedies has fueled speculation about whether disturbing Ötzi's resting place unleashed a supernatural curse.

Skeptics argue that the deaths are unrelated and statistically insignificant, given the number of people involved in the Iceman's discovery and study. Scientists continue to study Ötzi, uncovering insights into prehistoric life, including his diet, tools, and even his cause of death—a violent arrow wound.

The legend of Ötzi's curse endures, blending ancient mystery with modern intrigue. Whether a coincidence or a cautionary tale, the Iceman's story continues to captivate and mystify.

# THE MYSTERY OF THE DANCING FOREST

In a remote corner of Russia's Kaliningrad region lies a peculiar natural wonder known as the Dancing Forest. This grove of pine trees, located within the Curonian Spit National Park, has baffled scientists and visitors for decades. Unlike ordinary trees, the trunks here twist and spiral into bizarre shapes—loops, curls, and spirals—creating an otherworldly spectacle.

The forest's unusual appearance has sparked numerous theories. Some scientists attribute the phenomenon to a rare genetic mutation or unstable sandy soil that forces the trees to grow in irregular patterns as they seek stability. Others suggest it could be the result of wind

patterns or pest infestations that distorted the trees during their growth.

Beyond scientific explanations, the Dancing Forest has inspired folklore and mystical interpretations. Local legends claim the forest is enchanted, with the twisted trees symbolizing trapped spirits or supernatural forces at play. Some believe the area has unique energy fields, attracting spiritual seekers who say they feel a mysterious vibration when visiting the site.

Adding to the intrigue, the Dancing Forest is not alone in its strangeness. Similar twisted tree formations have been found in other parts of the world, such as the Crooked Forest in Poland, further deepening the mystery.

Despite the lack of a definitive explanation, the Dancing Forest continues to draw visitors from around the world, eager to witness its surreal beauty. Whether a natural anomaly, a scientific puzzle, or a portal to the mystical, it's a reminder of nature's ability to surprise and inspire awe.

# THE ENIGMA OF THE TAOS HUM

In the small town of Taos, New Mexico, a strange and persistent sound has puzzled residents and scientists for decades. Known as the Taos Hum, this low-frequency noise is described as a faint droning or rumbling, often compared to the sound of a distant diesel engine. While some hear it clearly, others remain completely oblivious, adding another layer of mystery to the phenomenon.

The Taos Hum first gained widespread attention in the early 1990s, when residents began reporting the noise to local authorities. Despite numerous investigations, including studies by scientists and engineers, the source of the hum has never been definitively identified.

It's particularly perplexing because the sound is often reported indoors and becomes less audible when outdoors.

Several theories have been proposed. Some suggest the hum could be caused by industrial equipment, natural geological activity, or low-frequency electromagnetic waves. Others speculate it may be linked to tinnitus, a condition affecting hearing. However, these explanations fail to account for why only a select group of people can hear the sound.

The more speculative ideas veer into the realm of conspiracy, with some attributing the hum to secret military projects, extraterrestrial activity, or even mass psychological phenomena. None of these theories, however, have provided concrete answers.

The Taos Hum remains an unsolved enigma, one that has drawn curious visitors, sound researchers, and paranormal enthusiasts to the area. Whether a natural phenomenon, a human-made anomaly, or something entirely unexplained, the hum continues to intrigue and frustrate, leaving us with more questions than answers.

# THE MYSTERY OF THE WOW! SIGNAL

On August 15, 1977, a powerful, unexplained radio signal was detected by astronomer Jerry R. Ehman while working on a SETI (Search for Extraterrestrial Intelligence) project at Ohio State University. The signal, originating from the constellation Sagittarius, lasted 72 seconds and was so unusual that Ehman wrote "Wow!" in the margin of the printout, giving the event its now-famous name.

The Wow! Signal stood out because of its intensity and narrow bandwidth, characteristics of a transmission not naturally produced in space. The signal came from a region of the sky with no known stars or planets capable of generating such a signal, adding to the intrigue.

Despite numerous follow-up observations, the signal was never detected again, deepening the mystery.

Theories about the Wow! Signal's origin range from natural phenomena, such as a comet or interstellar gas cloud, to more speculative ideas like extraterrestrial communication. In 2017, one researcher proposed that the signal might have been caused by a hydrogen cloud surrounding a comet, but this explanation has not been universally accepted.

SETI scientists have long sought signs of intelligent life in the universe, and the Wow! Signal remains one of the most compelling pieces of evidence to date. However, its transient nature and the lack of subsequent detections make it impossible to confirm its source.

The Wow! Signal continues to inspire debates, research, and even art, symbolizing humanity's quest to answer one of our most profound questions: Are we alone in the universe? Until another signal like it is discovered, the Wow! Signal remains an enigmatic whisper from the cosmos.

# THE LEGEND OF THE GREEN FLASH

For centuries, sailors and stargazers alike have whispered tales of the elusive "green flash," a phenomenon said to occur just as the sun sets or rises. Those lucky enough to witness it describe a fleeting burst of emerald light on the horizon—a moment so brief it's often dismissed as myth. But the green flash is real, though rare, and steeped in both science and lore.

The phenomenon occurs under specific atmospheric conditions. When the sun is near the horizon, its light passes through a thicker layer of the Earth's atmosphere. This bends (or refracts) the light, separating it into different colors, much like a prism. The green light is the last visi-

ble color to be refracted before the sun dips below or rises above the horizon, creating the momentary flash.

Sailors once believed the green flash was a sign of good luck or a divine message. In popular culture, it gained fame through Jules Verne's 1882 novel *Le Rayon Vert* (*The Green Ray*), where it symbolizes clarity and truth. Some even claim that witnessing the flash imparts wisdom or grants the ability to understand one's true feelings.

The rarity of the green flash adds to its mystique. Clear skies, a low, flat horizon (like over an ocean), and perfect timing are essential to see it. Even then, it lasts only a second or two, leaving many doubting their own eyes.

Whether as a scientific curiosity or a symbol of fleeting beauty, the green flash continues to captivate imaginations. It's a reminder of the wonders hidden in the ordinary cycles of nature, waiting to be noticed by those who seek them.

# THE CURSE OF THE WINCHESTER MYSTERY HOUSE

In San Jose, California, stands one of America's most peculiar architectural marvels: the Winchester Mystery House. Built by Sarah Winchester, heiress to the Winchester rifle fortune, the sprawling mansion is infamous for its bizarre design and the eerie legends that surround it.

The story begins in 1881, when Sarah's husband and infant daughter died, leaving her grief-stricken. According to legend, a medium told her that her family was cursed by the spirits of those killed by Winchester rifles. To appease these spirits, she was instructed to build a house—and to never stop building.

For the next 38 years, construction

on the mansion continued day and night. The result was a labyrinth of 160 rooms, 10,000 windows, and 2,000 doors, many of which lead to nowhere. Staircases ascend into ceilings, doors open to sheer drops, and corridors twist in every direction. Sarah's obsession with constant building and the house's chaotic layout have fueled speculation that she designed it to confuse or trap vengeful spirits.

Despite the legends, Sarah Winchester's true motives remain unclear. Some believe she was simply eccentric and used the project as a way to cope with her grief. Others suggest she was an innovative designer or a victim of con artists who exploited her wealth.

Today, the Winchester Mystery House is a popular tourist attraction, drawing visitors intrigued by its haunted reputation and architectural oddities. Whether the product of a curse or a unique vision, the mansion stands as a testament to one woman's enigmatic life and the stories we build to explain the unexplainable.

# THE EXPLODING WHALE OF OREGON

On November 12, 1970, the small coastal town of Florence, Oregon, became the site of one of the most bizarre and explosive events in history. A 45-foot, 8-ton sperm whale had washed ashore and begun to decay, filling the air with an unbearable stench. Unsure of how to dispose of the massive carcass, local authorities came up with an unusual solution: dynamite.

The Oregon Highway Division decided that blowing up the whale would be the quickest and most effective method of disposal. They believed the explosion would reduce the whale to small pieces, which seagulls and other scavengers could then clean up. Engineers calculated that

half a ton of dynamite would do the job.

On the day of the explosion, a crowd of curious onlookers gathered to watch the spectacle. When the dynamite was detonated, the blast was far more powerful than expected. Instead of scattering small pieces, it sent massive chunks of whale blubber raining down on the crowd and nearby vehicles. One piece flattened a car parked a quarter-mile away, though fortunately, no one was seriously injured.

The event quickly became a cautionary tale of overconfidence and poor planning. Footage of the explosion aired on local news and later went viral, cementing the exploding whale as a legendary example of human ingenuity gone hilariously wrong.

Today, the tale of the exploding whale remains a favorite piece of Oregon lore, serving as a humorous reminder that sometimes the simplest solutions are the best—and that nature doesn't always cooperate with our plans.

# THE GHOST ARMY OF WORLD WAR II

During World War II, the U.S. Army deployed one of its most unconventional units: the 23rd Headquarters Special Troops, better known as the Ghost Army. This top-secret unit was tasked not with combat but with deception, using elaborate illusions to mislead German forces. Their unique and daring operations saved thousands of lives and played a crucial role in the Allies' success.

The Ghost Army consisted of about 1,100 artists, designers, actors, and engineers. Their arsenal included inflatable tanks and airplanes, realistic sound effects, and fake radio transmissions. By combining these elements, the unit could create the illusion of entire divisions where

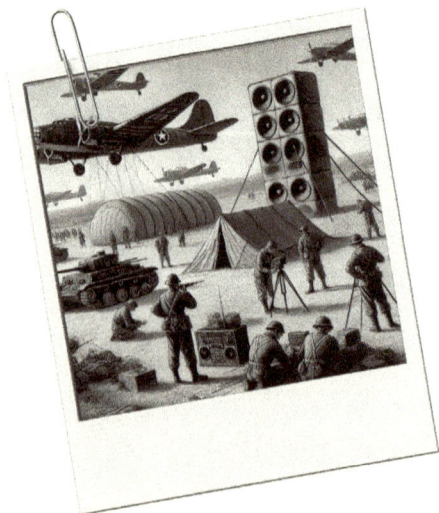

none existed. For example, they used giant speakers to broadcast the sounds of troop movements, tanks, and artillery from miles away, convincing the enemy of a massive Allied presence.

One of their most famous operations took place in 1944 during the Battle of the Bulge. The Ghost Army created a convincing decoy force to divert German troops away from the real Allied advance. Their efforts confused and delayed the enemy, allowing the Allies to regroup and gain the upper hand.

Despite their significant contributions, the Ghost Army's work remained classified for decades. It wasn't until the 1990s that their story became widely known, and in 2013, Congress awarded the unit a Congressional Gold Medal for their service.

The Ghost Army's creativity and ingenuity highlight the power of deception in warfare. Their legacy is a testament to the idea that battles can be won not only with strength but also with cleverness and imagination.

# THE BATTLE OF THE WHALESHIPS: A NAUTICAL MYSTERY

In 1820, the American whaleship *Essex* set sail from Nantucket on what should have been a routine whaling expedition. But the journey soon turned into a tale of survival so harrowing that it would inspire Herman Melville's *Moby-Dick*.

While hunting sperm whales in the South Pacific, the *Essex* crew spotted an enormous whale unlike any they had ever seen. It was nearly 85 feet long and, strangely, seemed to behave with a calculated malice. To the sailors' horror, the whale rammed the *Essex* twice, causing it to sink. The crew had little choice but to abandon ship, taking refuge in three small whale-

boats.

Adrift in the vast ocean, the men faced starvation, storms, and desperation. They tried to sail to safety but were pushed off course. After weeks at sea, their food supplies ran out, and the crew resorted to cannibalism—first consuming those who died naturally, and later drawing lots to sacrifice a crew member for survival.

Of the 20 men aboard the *Essex*, only eight survived to be rescued months later. Their horrifying ordeal became one of the most infamous maritime disasters of the 19th century, raising questions about humanity's resilience and the cruelty of the sea.

The story of the *Essex* is more than a nautical tragedy—it's a haunting reminder of the unpredictable forces of nature and the lengths to which humans will go to survive. It remains one of history's most harrowing tales of the sea, still evoking awe and chills centuries later.

# HY-BRASIL: THE ISLAND OF ETERNAL YOUTH

For centuries, sailors whispered tales of an enchanted island called Hy-Brasil, a land cloaked in mist and said to appear only once every seven years. Located somewhere off the western coast of Ireland, Hy-Brasil was believed to be a paradise—a place of eternal youth, riches, and advanced knowledge.

Early maps from the 14th to the 17th centuries included Hy-Brasil, often depicted as a circular island split by a river. Explorers, inspired by stories of a magical utopia, set out to find it. Some claimed to have glimpsed its shores, while others swore they had stepped foot on the island and encountered a mysterious civilization.

One of the most

famous accounts came from John Nisbet, a sailor in the 1670s. He reported that his crew was enveloped by a dense fog, and when it lifted, they found themselves on Hy-Brasil. The inhabitants, he claimed, were highly intelligent beings who bestowed knowledge and gifts upon the visitors before sending them on their way. Despite Nisbet's story, no concrete evidence of Hy-Brasil's existence ever emerged.

In modern times, Hy-Brasil has been linked to UFO lore. A British military intelligence officer claimed in 1980 that coordinates for a mysterious signal matched the supposed location of the mythical island. Some speculate that Hy-Brasil could be a misremembered sighting of real islands or even an ancient allegory for an unattainable dream.

Whether a fabled paradise, a cartographic error, or a tantalizing mystery, Hy-Brasil continues to captivate imaginations—a shimmering beacon of what might lie just beyond the horizon.

# RASPUTIN'S DEATH: THE MONK WHO DEFIED FATE

G rigori Rasputin, the mystic healer and confidant to Russia's last imperial family, lived a life shrouded in mystery. But it was his death that became the stuff of legend.

By 1916, Rasputin had made many enemies in St. Petersburg, thanks to his influence over Tsar Nicholas II and Tsarina Alexandra. Fearing he was leading the empire to ruin, a group of nobles led by Prince Felix Yusupov decided to assassinate him. But as the story goes, Rasputin didn't go down easily.

On the night of December 29, the conspirators lured Rasputin to Yusupov's palace under the guise of a social gathering. They served him

cakes and wine laced with cyanide. Remarkably, the poison seemed to have no effect. Growing desperate, Yusupov retrieved a pistol and shot Rasputin in the chest, leaving him for dead. Hours later, Rasputin reportedly revived, staggering out of the palace into the snowy courtyard.

Determined to finish the job, the assassins shot him again, then beat him mercilessly. Finally, they tied him up and threw him into the freezing Neva River. When Rasputin's body was recovered, his hands were outstretched as if he had tried to claw his way to the surface.

While modern historians question the accuracy of these details, Rasputin's death solidified his reputation as "The Mad Monk" who defied logic and death itself. His murder marked the beginning of the end for the Romanov dynasty, plunging Russia further into chaos and revolution.

Whether Rasputin was a mystic, a manipulator, or a misunderstood man, one thing is certain: his life and death remain one of history's most chilling and enigmatic tales.

# NOOR INAYAT KHAN: A SPY'S SILENT BRAVERY

During World War II, one of Britain's most courageous spies was a soft-spoken woman named Noor Inayat Khan. Born to an Indian Sufi mystic and an American mother, Noor was an unlikely candidate for espionage. Yet, she became a key figure in the French Resistance, fighting against Nazi occupation.

Noor joined Britain's Special Operations Executive (SOE) in 1942, a secret organization that trained agents to carry out sabotage and subversion behind enemy lines. Despite her gentle demeanor and pacifist upbringing, she quickly became one of their most skilled radio operators.

In 1943, Noor was sent to Paris

under the codename "Madeleine." Her mission: to transmit critical intelligence to the Allies. The work was dangerous, as the Nazis were adept at tracking radio signals. Many agents didn't survive long, but Noor evaded capture for months, tirelessly sending encrypted messages that helped coordinate Resistance efforts.

Unfortunately, Noor was betrayed by an informant. She was arrested by the Gestapo and subjected to brutal interrogations. Despite the torture, she refused to reveal any information, protecting her fellow operatives until the very end.

In 1944, Noor was executed at the Dachau concentration camp. Her final word, reportedly, was "Liberté."

Noor Inayat Khan's bravery and resilience remain an inspiration. She was posthumously awarded the George Cross, one of Britain's highest civilian honors, and the French Croix de Guerre. Her story reminds us that courage comes in many forms, and even the gentlest souls can make the greatest impact.

# THE FORGOTTEN CITY BENEATH THE WAVES: PAVLOPETRI

Beneath the turquoise waters off the coast of southern Greece lies Pavlopetri, one of the world's oldest submerged cities. Discovered in 1967, this Bronze Age marvel dates back over 5,000 years and offers an extraordinary glimpse into a civilization lost to time.

Unlike mythical Atlantis, Pavlopetri is very real. Archaeologists uncovered streets, houses, courtyards, and even what appears to be a drainage system—a rare find for its era. The city's layout suggests advanced urban planning, with evidence of trade and daily life etched into the seabed.

So, how did such a thriving settlement end up underwater? Most experts believe that a series of earthquakes and rising sea levels caused the city to sink around 1000 BCE. Despite its watery grave, Pavlopetri remains remarkably well-preserved, protected by layers of sand and sediment.

Modern technology has revealed even more secrets. Using 3D mapping and underwater drones, researchers have uncovered pottery, tools, and other artifacts that hint at the city's bustling trade network. The findings suggest that Pavlopetri was a significant hub in the ancient world, connecting cultures across the Mediterranean.

What makes Pavlopetri so fascinating isn't just its age but the stories it tells about the people who lived there. From fishermen mending nets to traders exchanging goods, life in Pavlopetri was likely not so different from ours—until the sea claimed it.

Today, Pavlopetri remains a haunting reminder of nature's power and a treasure trove for archaeologists. As the waves lap gently above its ruins, it silently whispers the tale of a world that time almost forgot.

# SCHRÖDINGER'S CAT: THE MAN IN A PARADOX

Few scientific thought experiments have captured the public's imagination like Schrödinger's cat. Devised in 1935 by Austrian physicist Erwin Schrödinger, this mental exercise was intended to highlight the bizarre implications of quantum mechanics. But what started as a critique has become one of the most iconic and perplexing symbols of science.

Here's how it goes: Imagine a cat placed inside a sealed box. Inside the box are a Geiger counter, a

radioactive atom, a vial of poison, and a hammer. If the atom decays—a random quantum event— the Geiger counter detects it, triggering the hammer to break the vial and release the poison, killing the cat. If the atom doesn't decay, the cat remains alive.

Now comes the paradox: Until someone opens the box to observe what happened, the cat exists in a state of quantum superposition—it's both alive and dead simultaneously. This strange concept stems from the idea that, at a quantum level, particles exist in multiple states until observed.

Schrödinger proposed the thought experiment to critique the Copenhagen interpretation of quantum mechanics, which suggested that reality only becomes definite when measured. In Schrödinger's eyes, applying this to everyday objects (like a cat) revealed the absurdity of such a notion.

Though Schrödinger's cat wasn't meant to be taken literally, it's become a powerful metaphor for the mysteries of quantum mechanics. The paradox still sparks debates among physicists and philosophers, illustrating the strange intersection of science and perception.

So, the next time you ponder life's mysteries, remember Schrödinger's cat—a thought experiment that left the world wondering whether reality itself is in the eye of the beholder.

# PENDLE HILL: ENGLAND'S WITCH TRIAL TRAGEDY

In 1612, a small village in Lancashire, England, became the epicenter of one of the most infamous witch trials in British history. Known as the Pendle Witch Trials, it saw twelve individuals accused of sorcery, leading to executions that would haunt the region for centuries.

The story begins with a young girl, Alizon Device, who cursed a pedlar after he refused her request for pins. Shortly after, the pedlar suffered a stroke, fueling rumors that Alizon had bewitched him. The accusations snowballed, implicating her family and neighbors, many of whom were already regarded as outsiders or troublemakers.

The accused

were rounded up and imprisoned in Lancaster Castle. Evidence was thin but damning, often based on hearsay or confessions extracted under duress. One of the most shocking witnesses was a nine-year-old girl, Jennet Device, who testified against her own family, sealing their fates.

In August 1612, the trial culminated in the execution of ten individuals, hanged for crimes they likely never committed. The Pendle Witches' fate became a chilling example of how fear and superstition could spiral out of control, tearing communities apart.

But the story doesn't end there. Pendle Hill remains shrouded in mystery, attracting ghost hunters and curious visitors. Many claim to feel a sinister presence or hear the whispers of those unjustly condemned. The legacy of the trials endures, a reminder of humanity's darker impulses and the devastating consequences of hysteria.

Today, the Pendle Witch Trials stand as a cautionary tale—a sobering reflection on the dangers of scapegoating and the enduring power of fear.

# THE AMBER ROOM: TREASURE LOST TO TIME

Imagine a room so magnificent it shimmered like gold, adorned with amber panels, gilded moldings, and mirrors reflecting a dazzling glow. This was the Amber Room, often called the "Eighth Wonder of the World." Created in 1701, this masterpiece was a gift from Prussia's King Frederick William I to Peter the Great of Russia, symbolizing friendship between their nations.

The Amber Room resided in the Catherine Palace near St. Petersburg, where it mesmerized visitors for over two centuries. But its story took a dark turn during World War II. In 1941, Nazi forces invaded the Soviet Union and looted the Amber Room. Despite attempts to hide it, the

Nazis dismantled the treasure and transported it to Königsberg Castle in Germany. Then, it vanished.

As the war ended and Allied forces closed in, the Amber Room seemingly disappeared without a trace. Did it succumb to Allied bombing? Was it hidden in a secret bunker, or spirited away by Nazi officials? To this day, its fate remains one of the greatest unsolved mysteries of World War II.

Over the years, treasure hunters, historians, and conspiracy theorists have scoured Europe for the Amber Room, spurred by tantalizing rumors and alleged sightings. In 2003, Russia unveiled a painstakingly reconstructed version of the room, but the original remains elusive.

The Amber Room's disappearance has captured imaginations for decades, blending history, art, and intrigue into a tale as luminous as the amber itself. Whether it lies buried beneath a forgotten castle or rests at the bottom of a Baltic Sea shipwreck, the legend of the Amber Room continues to shine brightly in the annals of mystery.

# THE VANISHING FORTUNE OF FORREST FENN

In 2010, eccentric art dealer Forrest Fenn announced a treasure hunt like no other. He claimed to have hidden a chest filled with gold coins, jewels, and other riches, worth over $2 million, somewhere in the Rocky Mountains. His only clue? A cryptic 24-line poem included in his memoir, *The Thrill of the Chase*.

The treasure hunt captured imaginations worldwide. Weekend adventurers, amateur sleuths, and full-time treasure hunters poured over Fenn's poem, trying to decode its meaning. Fenn encouraged the search, insisting the treasure was out there, waiting for the sharpest mind — or the boldest spirit — to find it.

But the hunt was not without

controversy. Over a decade, thousands scoured the Rockies, with some taking perilous risks. Tragically, five treasure hunters lost their lives during the search, sparking debates about the ethics of such a challenge. Critics demanded Fenn reveal the treasure's location to prevent further tragedies, but he refused, maintaining that the quest was a test of wit and determination.

Finally, in June 2020, Fenn announced that the treasure had been found. A man from Michigan had successfully solved the poem's riddle and discovered the chest. Yet, Fenn and the finder chose to keep the location and details a secret, fueling speculation and conspiracy theories. Some doubted the treasure ever existed, while others believed it had been secretly claimed years earlier.

Forrest Fenn passed away a few months later, taking with him the full story of his enigmatic treasure. Was it an elaborate riddle that rewarded the adventurous or a masterful hoax designed to inspire wonder? The mystery of Fenn's treasure remains as tantalizing as the quest itself. Would you have joined the hunt?

# THE MYSTERY OF THE SOMERTON MAN

In December 1948, an unidentified man was found dead on Somerton Beach near Adelaide, Australia. Dressed in a sharp suit and polished shoes, he lay slumped against a seawall with no obvious signs of violence. Authorities were baffled by the lack of identification and personal belongings—no wallet, no ID, not even labels on his clothes.

The case took a stranger turn when a tiny scrap of paper with the words "Tamam Shud" was dis-

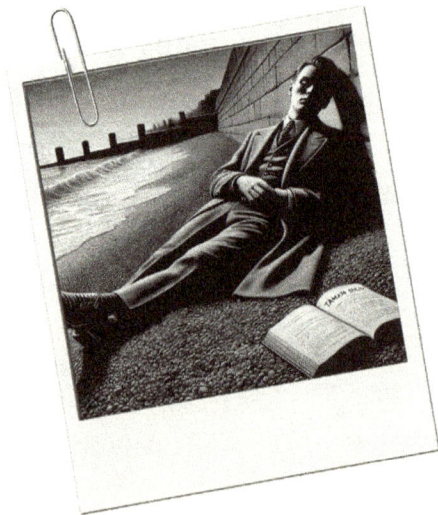

covered in a hidden pocket of his pants. The phrase, meaning "finished" or "ended" in Persian, was traced to a rare edition of *The Rubáiyát of Omar Khayyám*. Investigators eventually located a copy of the book in a stranger's car, which contained an incomplete phone number and a cryptic code scrawled inside.

The phone number led to a local nurse, who denied knowing the man but displayed visible distress upon seeing a bust of his face. Her connection to the case remains a subject of speculation, as does the nature of the coded message, which experts have yet to decipher.

Over the decades, theories about the Somerton Man have ranged from espionage to a tragic love story. Some believe he was a Cold War spy, citing the cryptic code as evidence of secret communications. Others think he was a jilted lover, his death a poetic nod to *The Rubáiyát*'s themes of fate and finality.

In 2021, DNA extracted from hair samples led to a possible identification: Carl "Charles" Webb, a Melbourne-born electrical engineer. But even with this lead, questions linger. Why was Webb in Adelaide? Who was he meeting? And what does the mysterious code mean?

The Somerton Man case remains one of Australia's most enduring enigmas, a riddle that tantalizes investigators and amateur sleuths alike.

# THE SILENT PIANIST'S HAUNTING LEGACY

In the early 1900s, a pianist named Dorian Green captivated audiences in Europe with his hauntingly beautiful performances. Known for his almost otherworldly skill, Dorian had one peculiar quirk—he never spoke a word, onstage or off. Audiences whispered about the silent virtuoso, whose fingers danced over the keys with supernatural precision.

But his fame came with eerie rumors. After Dorian performed in small towns, strange misfortunes seemed to follow. In one village, crops failed inexplicably; in another, an entire street of homes burned down without a discernible cause. People began to speculate that Dorian carried a curse, his music both a gift and a harbinger of

doom.

The mystery deepened when Dorian abruptly disappeared in 1913, vanishing after a concert in Vienna. He left no farewell, no trace—only his piano, abandoned in the concert hall. Authorities searched for him, but he was never seen again.

The intrigue didn't end there. Decades later, Dorian's piano turned up in a private collection, and those who played it reported hearing whispers in the silence between notes. One pianist swore he glimpsed a shadowy figure in a mirror while practicing on it. Others claimed the keys moved on their own, as if compelled by unseen hands.

Modern historians have tried to piece together Dorian Green's story, but his origins remain unclear. Was he a prodigy with a penchant for mystique or something more? The cursed pianist's life is as enigmatic as his music, leaving a haunting legacy that endures in whispers and ghostly melodies.

Dorian Green's tale reminds us that even the most beautiful art can carry a shadow, a mystery that lingers long after the music stops.

# BERMEJA: THE ISLAND THAT VANISHED

In the Gulf of Mexico, maps from the 16th century showed a curious little island named Bermeja. Described as a small, reddish landmass, Bermeja appeared on countless charts over centuries. But here's where it gets strange: by the 20th century, Bermeja had vanished without a trace.

During the 1990s, Mexican authorities desperately searched for the island. Why? Bermeja was crucial in defining Mexico's exclusive economic zone, an area rich in oil and gas reserves. If the island existed, Mexico's territorial claims would expand significantly. Yet despite advanced technology, aerial surveys, and extensive expeditions, not a single speck of Bermeja

could be found.

So, what happened to it? Some say Bermeja might never have existed—a cartographic error passed down through the ages. Others speculate it sank due to natural events like an earthquake or rising sea levels. But then the theories get wilder. A popular conspiracy suggests Bermeja was deliberately destroyed—perhaps bombed by a foreign government or erased from records to prevent Mexico from extending its oil-rich territory.

Even modern satellites haven't uncovered a definitive answer. The coordinates where Bermeja should be reveal nothing but open water.

The mystery of Bermeja remains unsolved. Was it an illusion of cartographers, a victim of nature, or something more sinister? To this day, the island—or the idea of it—continues to fuel debates, conspiracies, and a longing to uncover the truth about this lost piece of history.

Perhaps Bermeja's greatest legacy isn't its existence but the way it reminds us how maps, like legends, can shape the world—even when they lead to nowhere.

# THE CURSE OF THE CRYING BOY: A HAUNTING TALE

In the late 20th century, a peculiar painting began to surface in homes across the United Kingdom—a portrait of a tearful young boy. Known as *The Crying Boy*, this artwork became an unlikely bestseller. Yet, what seemed like a harmless piece of decor quickly gained a chilling reputation.

Stories emerged of homes that mysteriously caught fire, leaving everything in ashes—except for the painting. Firefighters reportedly found the unscathed portraits amidst the rubble, fueling whispers of a curse. As the tales multiplied, so did the fear surrounding the artwork. Was the painting truly cursed, or was it merely a coincidence?

Urban legends added eerie backstories. One claimed the boy in the painting was an orphan whose tragic life imbued the portrait with sorrowful energy. Another said the artist had made a deal with the devil, dooming anyone who displayed the painting.

In 1985, a UK tabloid stoked the flames of fear with sensational headlines about *The Crying Boy Curse*. Readers sent in accounts of their own fiery misfortunes, prompting thousands to destroy their copies in desperate attempts to avoid disaster.

Skeptics offered rational explanations, suggesting the paintings were printed on fire-retardant materials, but the legend persisted. Some even staged public burnings to rid their communities of the alleged hex.

Today, *The Crying Boy* is a collector's item, sought after for its mysterious past. Whether you believe in curses or not, one thing is certain: the painting's legacy remains as haunting as the tear-streaked face of the boy it depicts. Dare to hang it in your home? You might want to keep a fire extinguisher handy—just in case.

# SHRUNKEN HEADS: THE MYSTERY OF FACT OR FICTION

Deep within the Amazon rainforest, a gruesome tradition captivated Western imaginations—the creation of shrunken heads, or *tsantsas*. These eerie relics, crafted by the Shuar and Achuar peoples of Ecuador and Peru, were said to contain powerful spirits and served as symbols of victory in battle.

The process itself was as intricate as it was macabre. Warriors would remove the head of an enemy, peel back the skin, and discard the skull. The skin was then boiled, shrunk, and reshaped, with hot stones and sand used to maintain its lifelike appearance. Eyes and lips were sewn shut to trap the soul of the defeated, preventing it

from seeking revenge.

While the practice held deep spiritual and cultural significance, the arrival of Western explorers in the 19th century turned the *tsantsa* into a lucrative trade item. Foreign collectors, captivated by the bizarre artifacts, offered guns, tools, and money in exchange. This demand led to an unsettling market where counterfeit shrunken heads—crafted from animal hides or human remains stolen from morgues—flooded the market.

By the mid-20th century, international laws were enacted to prohibit the trade, but the fascination endures. Genuine *tsantsas* now reside in museums, where debates about cultural preservation and the ethics of displaying such artifacts continue.

For the Shuar and Achuar, the *tsantsa* was never just an oddity—it was a sacred object imbued with meaning. Today, they strive to reclaim the narrative, sharing the deeper truths behind a tradition often misunderstood and sensationalized.

So, the next time you see a shrunken head, remember: it's more than just a morbid curiosity. It's a piece of history, shrouded in mystery and layered with meaning.

# THE GHOST IN THE MACHINE: THE ENIGMA OF ELIZA

In the mid-1960s, an unlikely therapist emerged — not a human, but a computer program named ELIZA. Created by MIT researcher Joseph Weizenbaum, ELIZA was designed to simulate a conversation, using simple text-based exchanges. What started as a technical experiment quickly spiraled into something eerily profound.

ELIZA worked by mimicking a Rogerian psychotherapist, flipping user statements into questions.

For example, if you typed, "I feel sad," ELIZA might respond, "Why do you feel sad?" Simple enough, right? Yet, users found themselves pouring out their hearts to this digital confidante.

Here's where

it gets strange: many users formed deep emotional connections with ELIZA, believing they were communicating with something more than a machine. Weizenbaum himself was stunned when even his secretary asked for private time with ELIZA to discuss her problems. To him, it was a stark warning about humanity's tendency to project emotions onto machines.

But was ELIZA just a clever trick, or did it reveal something deeper about our minds? Psychologists and philosophers began debating whether meaningful connections could arise between humans and artificial intelligence. Was the program simply mirroring its users, or was it a glimpse into the future of digital empathy?

Fast forward to today, and ELIZA's legacy lives on in AI chatbots, digital assistants, and even therapy apps. While these technologies have advanced far beyond ELIZA's simplistic responses, the ghost in the machine lingers—reminding us of our hunger for connection, even with something non-human.

In a world increasingly intertwined with artificial intelligence, ELIZA's story poses a haunting question: how much of our humanity are we willing to share with machines? And just how much of it will they understand?

# THE VANISHING GOLD OF VICTORIO PEAK

In 1937, Doc Noss, a charming but eccentric adventurer, stumbled upon a cave in New Mexico's Victorio Peak. As he ventured into its dark recesses, he claimed to have discovered a treasure trove of gold bars—thousands of them. This find, potentially worth billions in today's currency, could have been the stuff of fairytales if not for what happened next.

Doc, determined to extract his newfound wealth, dynamited the entrance to widen it. But instead of creating an easier pathway, the explosion sealed the treasure behind tons of rock. Despite years of effort, Doc couldn't retrieve the gold. He shared tales of the treasure but was ultimately dismissed as a fraud. Then, in a bizarre twist, Doc

was mysteriously murdered in 1949, taking any secrets about the treasure's exact location to his grave.

But the story doesn't end there. Enter the U.S. Army. In the 1950s, Victorio Peak became part of a military testing range. Rumors flew that soldiers had stumbled upon the gold during training exercises. The government, however, vehemently denied finding anything.

Over the decades, numerous treasure hunters, including Doc's widow, Ova, sought permission to search the peak. Despite their efforts, no one could prove the existence of Doc's golden hoard. Speculation abounded: Had the Army secretly removed the gold? Did it ever exist at all?

Today, Victorio Peak remains an enigmatic desert mystery. The promise of unimaginable wealth, coupled with the peak's military restrictions, fuels conspiracy theories and keeps treasure hunters dreaming. Maybe the gold is still out there, hidden in the shadows of history, waiting for someone brave—or lucky—enough to claim it.

# THE SECRET SOCIETY OF THE BOHEMIAN GROVE

D eep in the redwood forests of California lies one of the most secretive and exclusive gatherings in the world: the Bohemian Grove. Each summer, this 2,700-acre retreat becomes the playground of the powerful and influential—U.S. presidents, global business leaders, and elite artists have all been counted among its members.

Founded in 1872 by a group of San Francisco journalists, the Bohemian Club initially sought to foster camaraderie among creative minds. But over the years, its membership shifted to include the rich and powerful, turning the Grove into a nexus of high society.

Here's where things get truly bi-

zarre. The Grove's annual two-week retreat kicks off with a peculiar ceremony known as the "Cremation of Care," in which members, clad in robes, gather around a massive owl statue to "symbolically burn" their worldly worries. Critics have called it eerie, even occult-like, while members insist it's all in good fun.

Despite the club's insistence on secrecy, rumors abound. Some say deals that shaped history were made under those towering redwoods—others whisper of strange rituals and political plots. In 2000, a journalist infiltrated the Grove and captured video footage of the "Cremation of Care," fueling conspiracy theories and public fascination.

What really happens at Bohemian Grove? Members remain tight-lipped, adhering to the club's motto: "Weaving spiders come not here," a warning to leave business at the gates. Whether it's an innocent retreat or something more sinister, the Grove's mystique has made it a perennial subject of intrigue.

As the saying goes, "What happens in the Grove, stays in the Grove." But one thing's certain: the world's most influential minds have found a peculiar sanctuary in the heart of those ancient redwoods.

# THE LOST COSMONAUTS: SILENT HEROES OF SPACE

When the Soviet Union launched Yuri Gagarin into orbit in 1961, he became the first human to journey into space—or so the official story goes. But whispers of lost cosmonauts, brave souls who ventured into the void before Gagarin and never returned, have fueled conspiracy theories for decades.

According to these tales, the Soviets, eager to claim global supremacy in the Space Race, sent un-recorded missions into orbit as early as the late 1950s. These missions allegedly ended in tragedy, with cosmonauts dying in the vacuum of space or burning up upon reentry. Fearing embarrassment, the Soviet Union reportedly

erased these names from history.

One compelling piece of evidence came from Italian amateur radio operators, the Judica-Cordiglia brothers. In 1960, they claimed to have intercepted a chilling transmission: a woman's voice pleading in Russian, "I am hot... I am hot... I see a flame." The recording, supposedly from a failed Soviet space mission, sparked worldwide curiosity. Was this a doomed cosmonaut, or just Cold War propaganda?

Skeptics argue there's no solid proof of these lost missions. NASA astronauts, such as Chris Kraft, have dismissed the idea as implausible. However, the secrecy of the Soviet space program and the high stakes of the Space Race leave just enough room for doubt.

Whether true or not, the stories of lost cosmonauts remind us of the immense risks pioneers faced to reach the stars. Could there be forgotten heroes floating in eternal silence above us? The truth remains as elusive as the stars themselves.

# THE BEAST OF GÉVAUDAN: A PREDATOR'S REIGN

In the remote mountains of 18th-century France, a terrifying creature unleashed a reign of terror. Between 1764 and 1767, the Beast of Gévaudan reportedly attacked over 100 villagers, killing many and leaving the survivors in fear of the wilderness.

The Beast was described as wolf-like but far larger, with reddish fur, a black stripe along its back, and an unusually powerful jaw. Eyewitnesses swore it wasn't an ordinary wolf. It was a monster. The attacks were gruesome, with victims often found decapitated or partially devoured.

The panic reached the court of King Louis XV, who sent professional hunters to eliminate the creature. Despite their efforts, the attacks continued. One hunter claimed to have killed a massive wolf, but the attacks resumed shortly after, leading to suspicions that more than one beast roamed the region.

The tale took a mysterious turn when a local marksman, Jean Chastel, reportedly killed the creature in 1767. Chastel used a musket loaded with a silver bullet—fueling legends that the Beast was no ordinary predator but something supernatural. After Chastel's kill, the attacks ceased, but questions remained.

Was the Beast a rogue wolf? An escaped exotic animal? Or something else entirely? Modern theories range from genetic mutations to a lion brought to France by a nobleman. Others speculate about human involvement, suggesting the Beast could have been a trained animal unleashed as part of a cruel game.

The Beast of Gévaudan remains an enigma—a chilling blend of historical fact and folklore that has inspired countless stories. Was it a monster of flesh and blood, or a darker figment of collective fear? Whatever the answer, its shadow still looms over the French countryside.

# KECKSBURG'S MYSTERY: THE SILVER STAR INCIDENT

On December 9, 1965, a fiery object streaked across the evening sky over six U.S. states and Canada, drawing hundreds of witnesses. Described as a blazing fireball with a metallic glow, the object crash-landed in the small town of Kecksburg, Pennsylvania. What came next has puzzled people for decades.

Locals rushed to the scene and reported seeing a bell-shaped craft partially buried in the woods. It was marked with strange, undecipherable symbols, like something out of a sci-fi movie. Military personnel arrived quickly, cordoning off the area and allegedly removing the object under a heavy tarp. Residents claimed

they were silenced, ordered to forget what they'd seen.

Officially, NASA later claimed the object was a Soviet satellite, Cosmos 96, that had re-entered the atmosphere. However, experts debunked this explanation, as the satellite had burned up hours earlier, far from Kecksburg. Other theories emerged: a meteor, a secret military experiment, or even an extraterrestrial craft.

In the years that followed, the Kecksburg incident became known as "Pennsylvania's Roswell." NASA files related to the event mysteriously vanished in 2009, further deepening the intrigue. Today, the small town proudly celebrates its cosmic mystery with annual UFO festivals, complete with a replica of the alleged craft.

Whether it was a Soviet relic, an alien visitor, or something entirely unknown, the Kecksburg incident continues to captivate imaginations, leaving us to wonder: what truly fell from the stars that winter night?

# THE BLACK ORLOV: A DIAMOND'S DARK CURSE

The Black Orlov, a mesmerizing 67.5-carat diamond, is said to carry a curse as dark as its smoky hue. Legend claims the gem was once the eye of a sacred Hindu idol in India, stolen by a monk whose act of desecration doomed the diamond—and anyone who possessed it.

After its theft, tragedy seemed to shadow the Black Orlov. In the 20th century, the diamond surfaced in Russia, where it was owned by Princess Nadia Vyegin-Orlov, from whom the gem takes its name. Both she and another owner reportedly leapt to their deaths, spurring whispers of a sinister connection.

To break the curse, the diamond was allegedly cut

into three pieces, each intended to dissipate its malevolent energy. The largest piece became the Black Orlov we know today, re-set into a platinum necklace surrounded by 108 smaller diamonds.

Despite its grim reputation, the Black Orlov has enjoyed a glamorous afterlife, gracing exhibitions and auctions, even making appearances at the Academy Awards. Today, it rests in private hands, far removed from its original place of worship.

The curse's true power remains a mystery. Was it an ancient retribution, a series of coincidences, or a tale spun to inflate the gem's mystique? Regardless, the Black Orlov's allure continues to dazzle and haunt, a reminder that some treasures come with a heavy price.

# THE LOST LIBRARY OF NINEVEH: A KING'S LEGACY

Imagine a treasure trove of wisdom so vast it could rival the famed Library of Alexandria. This was the Library of Ashurbanipal, the grand collection of the Assyrian king who ruled from the capital of Nineveh in the 7th century BCE. King Ashurbanipal was not your average ancient ruler; he prided himself on his literacy, a rare skill for kings of his time, and he sought to gather every bit of knowledge the ancient world had to offer.

The library housed thousands of clay tablets inscribed with cuneiform script, covering subjects like astronomy, mathematics, medicine, and mythology. It even contained the Epic of Gilgamesh, the world's oldest

176

known literary work. Ashurbanipal's ambition wasn't just to preserve knowledge—it was to dominate the intellectual realm of his era.

But when Nineveh fell to invading forces in 612 BCE, the library vanished beneath layers of rubble and time. For centuries, its existence was forgotten, until British archaeologist Austen Henry Layard rediscovered it in the mid-19th century during excavations of ancient Mesopotamian ruins.

Here's where the mystery deepens: despite the rediscovery, the library's full contents remain unknown. Thousands of tablets are still undeciphered, while others are fragmented. Scholars continue to piece together its secrets, unveiling glimpses of ancient Mesopotamian life and thought.

What remains of the Library of Ashurbanipal serves as a haunting reminder of the fragility of human knowledge. Was its destruction inevitable, or was it an omen of the price civilizations pay for neglecting their legacies? In Nineveh's ruins lies a cautionary tale of wisdom gained—and lost.

# THE PHANTOM TIME HYPOTHESIS: HISTORY'S GAP

What if the year wasn't 2025 but actually closer to 1728? Enter the *Phantom Time Hypothesis*, one of the most fascinating and controversial ideas in historical studies. Proposed by German historian Heribert Illig in the 1990s, this theory suggests that nearly three centuries of the early Middle Ages—from 614 to 911 CE—were completely fabricated.

Illig's claim is as bold as it is baffling: influential leaders like Holy Roman Emperor Otto III, Pope Sylvester II, and Byzantine Emperor Constantine VII allegedly colluded to manipulate the calendar. Why? To legitimize Otto III's reign by placing it at the symbolic year

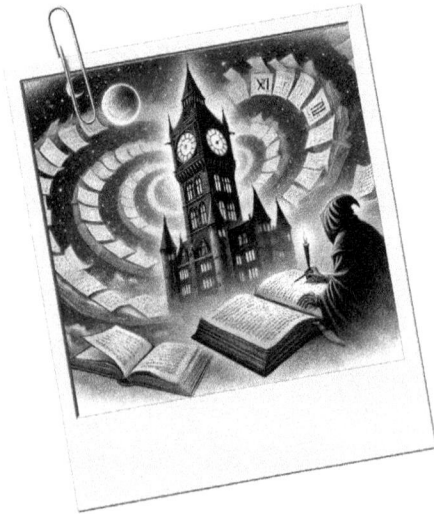

1000 CE. According to Illig, this grand scheme involved altering historical records, inventing entire events, and even fabricating iconic figures like Charlemagne.

The hypothesis leans on peculiar evidence. For instance, discrepancies in medieval architecture and a perceived scarcity of archaeological artifacts from the period raise questions. Illig also pointed to flaws in the Gregorian calendar reform of 1582, which adjusted for leap years. He argued the correction didn't fully align with actual astronomical observations—suggesting something was off in our chronology.

Mainstream historians reject the idea, citing solid records like astronomical events and reliable documentation from overlapping cultures. Still, the hypothesis forces us to think critically about how we measure time and understand history.

Could this be an elaborate hoax that survived centuries, or does it reveal cracks in our understanding of the past? The *Phantom Time Hypothesis* may not rewrite history, but it underscores the enduring allure of questioning the narratives we take for granted.

# THE TREASURE OF THE COPPER SCROLL MYSTERY

Imagine stumbling upon an ancient treasure map—but instead of "X marks the spot," it's a cryptic scroll made of copper, inscribed with detailed instructions leading to unimaginable wealth. That's exactly what researchers found in 1952 among the Dead Sea Scrolls: the enigmatic Copper Scroll.

Unlike its parchment and papyrus companions, the Copper Scroll stands out. Its text lists 64 locations said to conceal vast treasures of gold, silver, and other riches. We're talking about tons of precious metals—enough to make even the richest ancient kings envious.

The scroll, dated around the 1st century CE, is written in a peculiar mix of Hebrew and Arama-

ic. Scholars believe it was created during the Second Temple period, possibly by Jewish priests desperate to hide their temple treasures from the invading Romans.

But here's the catch: none of the listed treasures have ever been found. The scroll's directions are maddeningly vague. Phrases like "under the third step" or "in the cavity of the Old House of Garim" hint at secret locations, but without specific landmarks, treasure hunters have been left guessing for decades.

Some speculate that the treasures were already looted centuries ago. Others argue the scroll may have been a symbolic inventory, never tied to physical riches. And then there's the tantalizing possibility: the hoard remains hidden, waiting for someone clever—or lucky—enough to uncover it.

Fact or fantasy, the Copper Scroll fuels dreams of adventure and riches to this day. Perhaps it's not about finding the treasure, but the thrill of the hunt itself.

# THE MOA MYSTERY: NEW ZEALAND'S LOST GIANT

Imagine spotting a creature you're certain no longer exists. That's precisely what happened in the 20th century when rumors swirled about the reappearance of the giant, flightless moa—a bird believed to have gone extinct over 500 years ago.

The moa, native to New Zealand, was a colossal bird. Some species stood up to 12 feet tall and weighed over 500 pounds. For centuries, they roamed the forests and plains, with no natural predators—until humans arrived. The Maori hunted them extensively for food and used their massive bones and feathers for tools and ornamentation. By the 1400s, moas were declared extinct.

But in 1993, whispers of a possible moa sighting sent waves through the scientific and cryptozoological communities. Hikers in the remote forests of the South Island reported encountering a large, feathered bird unlike anything they'd ever seen. Similar claims had surfaced in the 19th and 20th centuries, but no conclusive evidence ever followed.

The possibility of a moa survival is tantalizing but controversial. New Zealand's dense and rugged wilderness could, in theory, hide a small population of these elusive creatures. Yet skeptics argue that such a large bird would need a significant food supply and population to avoid genetic bottlenecks, making long-term survival improbable.

Despite numerous expeditions, no moa has been found. All we have are tantalizing stories and blurred photographs. Was it mistaken identity, wishful thinking, or could the moa still haunt the shadows of New Zealand's forests?

For now, the moa remains a legend—a symbol of nature's resilience and a reminder of the mysteries that still lurk in the wild. Keep an eye out on your next hike—you never know what might cross your path!

# THE DEVIL'S FOOTPRINTS: A MYSTERIOUS TRAIL

On a frosty February night in 1855, the people of Devon, England, awoke to a puzzling sight. A single line of hoof-like tracks stretched for over 100 miles, weaving through snow-covered fields, crossing rivers, and climbing impossibly high walls. The bizarre part? The tracks appeared as if made by cloven hooves—sparking immediate whispers of supernatural origins.

Locals dubbed them "The Devil's Footprints." Rumors swirled that the Prince of Darkness himself had taken a moonlit stroll. Others suggested the marks were left by wandering kangaroos, though no one could explain how they got there. Even military experiments

were considered—perhaps a hot air balloon dragging something below it?

The tracks defied explanation. They meandered through the countryside, darting through haystacks and seemingly passing straight through solid objects. Was it a prank, an animal, or something far more sinister?

Though theories abound, the truth remains elusive. Over 150 years later, the Devil's Footprints endure as one of the most perplexing unsolved mysteries of the Victorian era.

# THE FORGOTTEN FORTRESS
# OF THE SKY

Deep within the frozen wilderness of the Arctic, lies a towering enigma—Svalbard's forgotten sky fortress. During the Cold War, this isolated vault wasn't just a place of icy wonder but a potential last refuge of humanity. Known as the **Doomsday Vault**, it's far more than just a treasure trove of seeds.

Carved into a mountainside on the Svalbard archipelago in 2008, this global seed vault stores samples of nearly every known crop on Earth, sealed in permafrost and steel. Its purpose? To ensure humanity's survival in the face of a nuclear winter, catastrophic climate change, or any apocalyptic event.

But here's where the mystery deepens: whispers of a hidden second vault persist. Unlike the seed repository, this secretive bunker is rumored to hold biological specimens—DNA of countless species, including humans. Conspiracy theories swirl about its real purpose. Some claim it's an ark for cloning in case of a species wipeout, while others suggest it's a repository for military bio-weapons.

Strange occurrences fuel the intrigue. In 2017, unusually high Arctic temperatures caused minor flooding at the entrance. A glitch? Or something more ominous? Visitors and researchers often report unsettling sensations near the vault, as though the very air vibrates with secrets.

What remains undeniable is the immense significance of Svalbard. The Doomsday Vault symbolizes hope, resilience, and humanity's determination to endure. Yet, its icy corridors may conceal more than seeds—perhaps the blueprint for a second chance at existence.

So, is this fortress of the sky merely a monument to human foresight, or a Pandora's box waiting to be opened? The icy silence keeps its secrets frozen—for now.

# THE HEADLESS VALLEY: CANADA'S HAUNTING MYSTERY

D eep within Canada's Northwest Territories lies the Nahanni Valley, a breathtaking expanse of rugged cliffs, hot springs, and roaring rivers. But beneath its natural beauty lurks a chilling mystery: a place so steeped in eerie tales and unexplainable disappearances that locals call it the Valley of Headless Men.

The legend begins in the early 20th century, when

prospectors flocked to the Nahanni River in search of gold. Among them were the McLeod brothers, who vanished without a trace in 1908. Months later, their decapitated remains were discovered near the riverbanks, fueling whispers of a vengeful curse. Over the decades, others met similar fates—headless and abandoned in the wilderness.

Stories of supernatural forces abound. Indigenous Dene tribes speak of "Naha," a mythical tribe of warriors said to guard the valley with deadly precision. Others claim the region is haunted by malevolent spirits or secretive mountain men protecting hidden treasures.

Modern explorers are drawn to the Nahanni's unspoiled beauty, but its dangers are real. Jagged cliffs, unpredictable rapids, and extreme weather have claimed countless lives. Even today, the valley resists explanation, shrouded in an aura of mystery and fear.

Is the Nahanni Valley cursed, or is its brutal wilderness simply unforgiving to the unwary? Whatever the truth, the Valley of Headless Men holds its secrets tightly—guarding them, perhaps, for eternity.

# COSTA RICA'S STONE SPHERES: ANCIENT ENIGMA

D eep in the jungles of Costa Rica lies a mystery that has puzzled archaeologists, historians, and explorers for decades: perfectly round stone spheres. These peculiar artifacts, known as "Las Bolas," range in size from a few inches to over eight feet in diameter, some weighing several tons. What makes them so intriguing is their near-perfect shape, achieved with remarkable precision.

The spheres were first documented in the 1930s when workers clearing banana plantations stumbled upon them. Made from a type of igneous rock called granodiorite, these spheres are not naturally occurring. They were painstakingly sculpted, but how and why remains a question

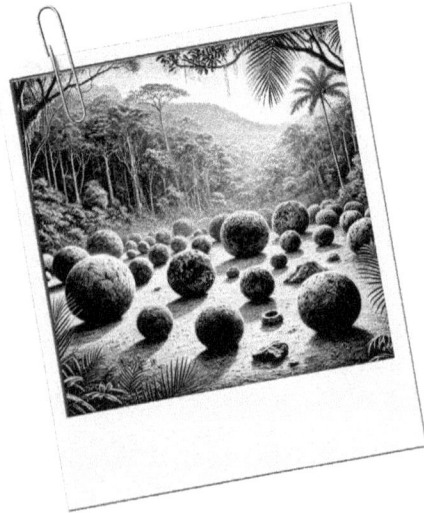

for the ages.

Some believe the spheres were created by the Diquís people, an ancient civilization that inhabited the region before the Spanish conquest. The Diquís left no written records, leaving the spheres as their enigmatic legacy. Were they markers for celestial navigation, symbols of power, or representations of the cosmos? No one knows for certain.

Over time, wild theories have emerged. Some suggest the spheres were created with advanced technology lost to history, while others point to extraterrestrial involvement. Adding to the mystery, many of the spheres were found in alignment with astronomical phenomena or arranged in complex patterns.

Sadly, many of the spheres have been moved or damaged over the years, making it even harder to unlock their secrets. Today, they stand as a UNESCO World Heritage Site, a testament to the ingenuity and artistry of an ancient people—and a reminder of how much we still have to learn about our past.

Are they symbols of power? Cosmic maps? Or messages to the stars? The Stone Spheres of Costa Rica challenge us to keep searching for answers.

# PATAGONIA'S VANISHING LAKE: NATURE'S MAGIC ACT

In southern Chile's Patagonia region, nestled in the pristine wilderness of the Andes, lies—or rather, once lay—a lake that confounded scientists and explorers alike. Known as Lake Cachet II, it wasn't just a picturesque glacial lake; it was an enigma.

In May 2007, locals and scientists alike were stunned when Lake Cachet II simply vanished overnight. One day, it was a sprawling body of water, holding enough to fill 4,000 Olympic swimming pools. The next morning, it was gone, replaced by a desolate, muddy basin. The event left more than just dry land—it left a mystery.

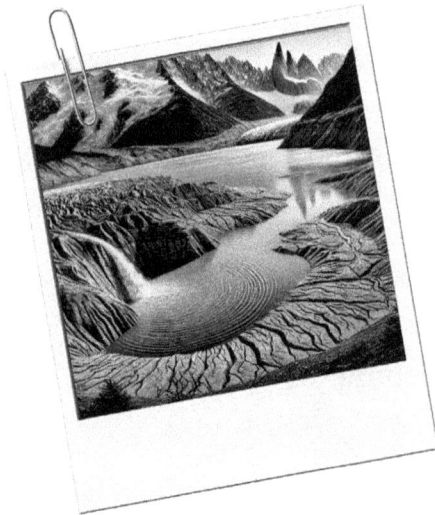

What could cause an entire lake to disappear so suddenly? The answer lies beneath the surface—literally. Cachet II sits atop an intricate network of tunnels within the nearby Colonia Glacier. Under the right conditions, these ice tunnels can drain the lake entirely in a dramatic event known as a glacial lake outburst flood. In just hours, the water from Cachet II flowed into these tunnels and gushed into the Baker River, raising water levels downstream.

What's fascinating is that this wasn't a one-time event. Lake Cachet II has since disappeared and reappeared multiple times, depending on weather patterns, glacier melt rates, and pressure changes in the surrounding ice. This phenomenon has transformed the lake into a living, breathing entity of nature's making.

The vanishing act of Lake Cachet II serves as a striking reminder of the fragile balance of Earth's ecosystems. It's a story of nature's power and unpredictability, one that continues to awe scientists and adventurers alike.

How can something so immense simply cease to exist—only to return again? The disappearing lake of Patagonia is a mystery that challenges our understanding of the natural world.

# THE CURSE OF PELE: HAWAII'S WRATH

awaiian mythology is rich with gods and goddesses, but none are as fiery as Pele, the goddess of volcanoes and fire. Revered as both a creator and a destroyer, Pele is said to have formed the Hawaiian Islands with her volcanic fury. But this fiery deity isn't just known for her geological handiwork—she's infamous for her curse.

Legend has it that taking lava rocks, sand, or any natural artifact from Hawaii as a souvenir comes with dire consequences. The curse of Pele is said to bring misfortune, bad luck, and even tragedy to those who defy her sacred land. Tourists often dismiss the tale as mere superstition—until things start to go wrong.

194

Over the years, thousands of remorseful visitors have mailed back rocks, sand, and shells to Hawaii's national parks, begging for forgiveness. Some letters recount a string of inexplicable accidents, financial ruin, or strained relationships. While skeptics chalk it up to coincidence, many believe it's the wrath of Pele, punishing those who disrespected her domain.

Pele's curse has become so well-known that Hawaiian park authorities routinely deal with "lava rock return" packages. They've even had to set up special procedures to catalog and return the natural artifacts to their rightful place.

While there's no scientific proof of the curse, the stories are compelling enough to make most think twice before pocketing a piece of paradise. Whether or not you believe in Pele's retribution, one thing is certain: the Hawaiian Islands are a sacred and powerful place, and their natural beauty deserves respect.

So, the next time you're tempted to take a rock as a keepsake, remember: Pele is always watching, and she doesn't forgive lightly.

# THE BAGHDAD BATTERY: ANCIENT POWER UNVEILED

I magine this: an artifact resembling an ancient battery, discovered in the ruins of Baghdad, Iraq. Dubbed the "Baghdad Battery," this curious relic has sparked debates for decades. Dating back over 2,000 years, it consists of a clay jar, a copper cylinder, and an iron rod. When filled with an acidic liquid, such as vinegar or lemon juice, the jar is capable of generating an electrical charge.

The artifact is attributed to the Parthian Empire, a civilization not typically associated with advanced technology. This raises the question: what purpose could an ancient battery serve? Some theorize it was used for electroplating metals—coating objects with gold or silver

through an electric current. Others suggest it had ceremonial or medicinal uses, perhaps for shocking patients to cure ailments, a practice surprisingly similar to later medical traditions.

Skeptics argue that the Baghdad Battery might not be a battery at all but merely a storage vessel. Yet, experiments replicating its design confirm its potential as a primitive power source.

Adding to the mystery, no written records explain its use, leaving researchers to rely on speculation. If it truly was a battery, it would represent an extraordinary leap in ancient engineering—a technology that seemingly vanished for centuries before resurfacing in modern times.

The Baghdad Battery challenges our assumptions about ancient civilizations and their ingenuity. Were they closer to unlocking the secrets of electricity than we imagined? Or is this artifact simply a misunderstood relic of a forgotten culture?

As we continue to uncover the mysteries of the past, the Baghdad Battery stands as a testament to human curiosity and invention, proving that history still holds plenty of surprises.

# THE NAZCA LINES: MYSTERIES IN THE DESERT

Scattered across the arid plains of southern Peru lies one of the world's greatest archaeological enigmas: the Nazca Lines. These vast geoglyphs, etched into the desert floor, have captivated and baffled scientists and adventurers alike for over a century.

From birds with wingspans stretching hundreds of feet to abstract shapes and humanoid figures, the Nazca Lines are so large they can only be fully appreciated from the sky. But here's the twist—these designs were created over 1,500 years ago, long before flight was even a concept. How did the Nazca people, an ancient civilization, create these enormous and intricate works of art with such precision?

Some research-

ers suggest they used rudimentary tools and simple geometry, but the purpose of the lines is another mystery. Were they ceremonial paths? Astronomical markers? Messages to their gods? Or perhaps, as some more imaginative theorists claim, they were landing strips for alien visitors.

What makes the lines even more remarkable is their survival. Despite centuries of exposure to harsh desert conditions, the lack of wind and rain in the region has kept them largely intact, as though the earth itself conspires to preserve their secrets.

In recent years, drones and satellite technology have uncovered even more lines, including new designs of snakes and cats, proving there's still much to learn. Yet, despite all our advances, the Nazca Lines remain a tantalizing riddle—a blend of human ingenuity and ancient mystery that continues to spark wonder across generations.

# THE CRYING STONES OF BOILING RIVER

Deep in the Peruvian Amazon lies a river so surreal it feels like a fable: the Shanay-Timpishka, also known as the Boiling River. Flowing for nearly four miles, its waters can reach temperatures of up to 200°F—hot enough to scald flesh and claim the lives of unsuspecting creatures that fall in.

The river's name translates to "boiled by the heat of the sun," but the truth is far more enigmatic. Scientists once thought such geothermal phenomena only occurred near volcanic activity, yet the Boiling River is hundreds of miles from the nearest volcano. Its origins remained a mystery until researchers discovered deep underground fault lines channeling scalding water to the

surface—a geological wonder hidden in plain sight.

Yet science only tells part of the story. For the local Asháninka people, the river holds sacred significance. Legends speak of spiritual healers and the cries of the river stones—rocks said to emit eerie wails as they are boiled alive. These cries, according to myth, are warnings from the Earth to respect its power.

The Boiling River isn't just a natural curiosity; it's a fragile ecosystem. Tiny creatures have adapted to survive in these extreme waters, while the surrounding rainforest provides a unique backdrop for one of Earth's rarest marvels.

To stand on its banks is to witness a living contradiction: a river that flows with deathly heat but sustains a delicate balance of life, legend, and mystery. The Boiling River remains a stark reminder of the Earth's untamed and hauntingly beautiful secrets.

# THE CRYING CAT CURSE: A STATUE'S OMINOUS LEGACY

N estled in a quiet Japanese village stands an unassuming stone statue of a cat, its surface weathered and its expression eerily mournful. Known locally as *Neko Namida*—the Crying Cat—this statue is steeped in an unsettling legend: anyone who dares to move or disrespect it invites misfortune.

The tale begins centuries ago when the statue was said to have been carved by a grieving artisan whose beloved cat saved him from a fire but perished in the

process. To honor its memory, the artisan created the statue, which wept mysteriously as it was completed. Villagers began to notice that anyone who tried to relocate the statue experienced a string of bad luck—crops failed, houses burned, and even illnesses spread mysteriously. Over time, the villagers built a shrine around it, leaving offerings to appease its spirit.

Despite the warnings, there were skeptics. In 1963, a wealthy landowner dismissed the legend as superstition and ordered the statue removed to expand his estate. Within weeks, his fortune dwindled as business deals collapsed, and a freak landslide destroyed his home. The statue was later found undamaged in the debris, returned to its original spot by frightened locals.

Even in modern times, the Crying Cat's curse persists. In 2010, a tourist reportedly mocked the statue, taking a photo while pretending to cry. Days later, his camera inexplicably shattered, and he narrowly escaped a serious accident. Local authorities now warn visitors to treat the statue with respect, citing both cultural significance and the eerie pattern of events.

The Crying Cat remains a curious enigma—a silent guardian, a harbinger of misfortune, or perhaps, just a relic with a remarkable story to tell. Dare you visit it?

# THE PHANTOM ISLAND OF SANDY: A MYSTERY

For centuries, sailors and explorers told tales of a mysterious island called Sandy. It appeared on maps and charts between Australia and New Caledonia, a tiny speck in the Pacific Ocean, first recorded by Captain James Cook in the 18th century. Over time, the island became a fixture of cartographic knowledge, included in official nautical charts and atlases. But here's the twist: Sandy Island didn't exist.

In 2012, a team of Australian scientists aboard the research vessel RV Southern Surveyor embarked on an expedition to this elusive landmass. Guided by maps and GPS, they arrived at the exact coordinates where Sandy Island was supposed to be. Instead of a sandy

beach or rugged terrain, they found nothing but open ocean, 4,500 feet deep.

The scientists were baffled. How could an island persist on maps for over 200 years without ever existing? Theories quickly emerged. Some suggested it was a simple cartographic error, perpetuated over centuries as maps were copied and recopied. Others speculated it might have been a transient pumice raft formed by volcanic activity, later dispersed by the ocean currents.

Sandy Island was officially erased from modern maps and databases after the 2012 expedition. However, the mystery lingers. Why was the island so firmly believed in the first place? And how did it remain unquestioned for so long?

The story of Sandy Island reminds us that even in the age of satellites and GPS, the vastness of our planet still holds room for illusions, myths, and mysteries. It's a testament to the power of human storytelling—and a gentle nudge to keep questioning the maps we follow.

# AMELIA EARHART'S DISAPPEARANCE IN AVIATION

A melia Earhart, a trailblazer in aviation and a symbol of fearless ambition, disappeared without a trace on July 2, 1937, during her attempt to circumnavigate the globe. Her plane vanished over the Pacific Ocean near Howland Island, leaving the world to wonder: what happened to Amelia Earhart?

Her Lockheed Electra aircraft, co-piloted by navigator Fred Noonan, was last heard from when she radioed a distress call, reporting that she was low on fuel and unable to locate the tiny island she was aiming for. Despite an unprecedented search effort by the U.S. Navy, involving ships, planes, and even local islanders, no conclu-

sive evidence of her fate was found.

Theories abound. Some believe Earhart's plane crashed into the ocean and sank, its wreckage still resting on the seabed. Others suggest she may have landed on an uninhabited island, such as Nikumaroro, where artifacts like a possible fragment of her plane and a woman's shoe have been discovered.

More sensational theories propose she was captured by the Japanese and held as a spy during the prelude to World War II. Some even claim she returned to the U.S. under an assumed identity.

Amelia Earhart's story remains one of aviation's most captivating mysteries, sparking endless fascination and debate. Expeditions continue to scour the Pacific, armed with modern technology, but her ultimate fate eludes us.

Her disappearance is not just a puzzle—it's a story of human curiosity and the relentless quest for answers. Whether her resting place lies beneath the ocean or in an unmarked grave, Earhart's legacy as a pioneering aviator and an enduring icon of courage continues to soar.

# THE ETERNAL FLAME
# MYSTERY AT CHESTNUT RIDGE

D eep in the forests of Chestnut Ridge, Pennsylvania, a natural marvel defies logic and stirs intrigue. Known as the Eternal Flame, this small, flickering fire burns brightly from within a rocky grotto. What makes it extraordinary? It's fueled by a continuous seepage of natural gas emerging from cracks in the rock—a phenomenon that science struggles to fully explain.

The Eternal Flame, nestled amidst a serene waterfall, is not the only natural gas seep in the world. However, its perpetual nature is unique. While other flames sputter and die without human intervention, this fiery beacon appears to burn without end, a literal torch passed

down by nature itself.

Legends abound about its origins. Some say Native Americans lit the flame centuries ago, believing it to be a portal to the spirit world. Others claim it's a gift from the gods, a divine signal of the earth's living energy. Scientists, however, have a more grounded explanation: methane-rich shale beneath the surface emits gas through fissures, providing a steady fuel source. But here's the catch—most methane seeps can't sustain flames at this level due to insufficient gas pressure.

The Eternal Flame remains a geological puzzle, a balancing act of natural gas flow, perfect oxygen levels, and a mysterious spark. Visitors who trek to see it are often struck by its otherworldly allure, a glowing symbol of the earth's hidden wonders.

Whether it's a scientific curiosity or a mystical phenomenon, the Eternal Flame continues to burn, captivating the minds and imaginations of those who seek it out.

# THE LEGEND OF THE MAN WHO LIVED IN A LIBRARY

D eep in Lisbon, Portugal, a man named Fernando Pessoa lived a life so intertwined with books that it became the stuff of legend. Known as one of the greatest modernist poets, Pessoa's real genius lay in the world he built—not through fiction, but through an uncanny ability to embody entire personalities, complete with their own writing styles, philosophies, and life stories.

Pessoa didn't just write under pseudonyms; he created "heteronyms." These were fully fleshed-out characters, each with distinct identities, professions, and even astrological charts. There was Alberto Caeiro, a pastoral poet who loved simplicity; Ricardo Reis, a stoic physi-

cian with a flair for odes; and Álvaro de Campos, a flamboyant, Whitman-inspired futurist.

But here's the kicker: Pessoa claimed he wasn't creating these personas; he was "discovering" them, as if channeling voices from another dimension. He often wrote as if these heteronyms were real people living inside his head, conversing and arguing with him. His literary "family" was so extensive that scholars still haven't cataloged all their works.

Pessoa's apartment, stuffed with books and manuscripts, was a labyrinth of creativity. After his death in 1935, a wooden trunk was found in his room, crammed with over 25,000 unpublished pieces of writing—a treasure trove of poetry, essays, and bizarrely vivid journal entries.

Today, Pessoa's legacy isn't just his work; it's the mysterious way he lived. Was he a literary genius, a man with dissociative identities, or something else entirely? No one knows for sure, but his world—a world of words within words—remains a literary enigma, forever inviting readers to get lost in its maze.

# CONCLUSION

Congratulations! You've journeyed through *100 Mind-Blowing Stories* and explored the strange, the surprising, and the downright unbelievable. From curious mysteries to forgotten histories, this collection has shown just how fascinating and unpredictable our world can be.

But here's the thing about curiosity—it's a never-ending adventure. For every story you've read, there are countless more waiting to be discovered. Maybe this book has sparked your imagination or inspired you to dig deeper into a topic that caught your eye. Or perhaps it's simply reminded you of the joy of learning something new, no matter how unexpected.

The truth is, the world is full of astonishing tales, and they don't all require a time machine or an ancient map to uncover. Sometimes, all it takes is an open mind and a willingness to ask, "What if?"

So as you close this book, don't think of it as the end. Think of it as a starting point—a collection of breadcrumbs leading to even more stories, wonders, and mysteries that are just waiting for someone as curious as you to find them.

Until next time, stay curious, stay adventurous, and remember: the best stories are the ones you share.

# ACKNOWLEDGEMENTS

Creating *100 Mind-Blowing Stories* has been a whirlwind of curiosity, caffeine, and moments of awe. While my name might be on the cover, this book wouldn't exist without the inspiration, support, and contributions of so many amazing people.

First, a heartfelt thank you to every history buff, storyteller, and trivia enthusiast who has ever shared an incredible tale. Your passion for the extraordinary is contagious, and this book is a testament to the wonders you've uncovered.

To my family and friends, who patiently listened to my excitement about emus, ghost ships, and ancient mysteries—you deserve a medal. Your encouragement (and willingness to nod along) kept me motivated every step of the way.

A huge shoutout to my readers—you're the real stars of this journey. Whether you're here for a laugh, a gasp, or a mind-blowing fact to share at your next dinner party, this book is for you. Your curiosity is what makes storytelling so rewarding.

And finally, to the universe itself—thanks for being

so wonderfully weird. You've given us a world filled with astonishing stories, and I'm grateful every day for the chance to share just a few of them.

Here's to curiosity, wonder, and all the incredible stories still waiting to be told.

# ABOUT THE AUTHOR

Felix Grayson is the creator of the 100 Mind-Blowing series — a fast-growing collection of books and audiobooks packed with the world's wildest stories, weirdest facts, and most fascinating moments. From ancient civilizations and scientific oddities to legendary sports upsets and real-life mysteries, Felix brings together the kind of tales that make you say, "Wait… that really happened?"

Fueled by a relentless curiosity and love of storytelling, Felix has dedicated his work to exploring the strange, the surprising, and the utterly unforgettable. Each title is a hand-picked journey through history, science, pop culture, and beyond — crafted to amaze, entertain, and spark wonder in curious minds of all ages.

With a writing style that blends clarity, energy, and a touch of humor, Felix turns trivia into page-turners and facts into unforgettable adventures. His goal?

To make knowledge fun again — and to remind us all that truth is often stranger (and cooler) than fiction.

When not researching bizarre true stories or mapping out new titles, Felix enjoys reading old novels, wandering offbeat museums, and sipping coffee while pondering the unexplained. on.

www.ingramcontent.com/pod-product-compliance
Lightning Source LLC
Chambersburg PA
CBHW031123020426
42333CB00012B/199